What the Bible *Really* Says

AFTER LIFE

DOUGLAS CONNELLY

InterVarsity Press
Downers Grove, Illinois

InterVarsity Press® is the book-publishing division of InterVarsity Christian Fellowship®, a student movement active on campus at hundreds of universities, colleges and schools of nursing in the United States of America, and a member movement of the International Fellowship of Evangelical Students. For information about local and regional activities, write Public Relations Dept., InterVarsity Christian Fellowship, 6400 Schroeder Rd., P.O. Box 7895, Madison, WI 53707-7895.

All Scripture quotations, unless otherwise indicated, are taken from the HOLY BIBLE, NEW INTER-NATIONAL VERSION®. NIV®. Copyright ©1973, 1978, 1984 by International Bible Society. Used by permission of Zondervan Publishing House. All rights reserved.

Cover illustration: Roberta Polfus
ISBN 0-8308-1648-8

Printed in the United States of America ∞

Library of Congress Cataloging-in-Publication Data

Connelly, Douglas, 1949-
    After life: what the Bible really says/Douglas Connelly.
      p.   cm.
    Includes bibliographical references and indexes.
    ISBN 0-8308-1648-8 (alk. paper)
    1. Future life—Biblical teaching.   2. Death—Biblical teaching.
  I. Title.
BS680.F83C64   1995
236'.2—dc20   95-22959
                                     CIP

16	15	14	13	12	11	10	9	8	7	6	5	4	3	2	1
07	06	06	05	04	03	02	01	00	99	98	97	96	95		

*To the men, women and children
of Cross Church,
my church family and my friends*

Acknowledgments

I've dedicated this book to the congregation I am privileged to pastor. The people who make up Cross Church love me, encourage me, pray for me and defend me. They are one of God's great blessings in my life.

Karen, my wife of twenty-five years, has been a wonderful motivator and support for me. She blesses my life every day. Kim, Kevin and Kyle add to that richness.

I want to thank Cindy Bunch-Hotaling at InterVarsity Press for her help and guidance. Every writer should be blessed with such an excellent editor.

My thanks also go to Jan Lund, who helped me meet some very tight deadlines with her expert word-processing skills.

Finally, I am grateful for seven men who hold me up and keep me accountable: Tom Skaff and Steve Aikman at our breakfast meetings; Matt Johnson, Ken Gilbert, Bill Sobey, Rich Tesner and Dick Adomat every Sunday. You will never know, guys, what an encouragement you are to me.

Chapter 1

I'M AFRAID OF DYING!

*M*y *first encounter with death came when I was a young teen-*ager. I went with my pastor father to the hospital to visit a woman from our church. She didn't talk much while we were there but seemed glad to see us as she squeezed our hands and smiled thinly. After a few minutes of conversation, my father ended our visit with prayer. As he prayed, I heard the woman give a short gasp and then a deep sigh. Her hand fell limp in mine. I looked up, and I knew something had changed. While we prayed, this dear saint of God had died.

My first response was fear. My father, however, was calm and reassuring. "It's all right," he said. "She has gone home to heaven." He gently touched the woman's cheek and pressed the call button for the nurse. I'm glad my father didn't leave me alone in that room, but I'm also glad he didn't send me outside.

That experience and my father's peaceful response prepared me to see death close-up many times since then. I've seen people die well, and I've seen a few die poorly. I face my own mortality every time I look into a casket.

Death always calls up questions: What happens *as* we die— and *after* we die? Where have our loved ones gone? Are they happy? Are they aware of us? Do they know how much we miss them?

While a lot of people claim to have the answers to these and other questions about death, Christians, more than any others, have a reliable source to turn to. That person's name is Jesus Christ. We can trust his word completely, for not only did he die and enter into life beyond the grave, he returned to this life in an awesome resurrection. In the record of his experience and in the instruction of his Word, the Bible, we can find the truth about death and what lies beyond it. Whether we find comfort or terror in that truth depends on our response to Jesus, who died in our place and came alive again so that we might have life after death.

Approaching Death as a Christian

If you want to be left alone at a party or social gathering, start asking people what they think the experience of death will be like. Your friends will soon find plenty of reasons to avoid you!

While everyone knows that death is inevitable, we aren't very comfortable talking about it. But that doesn't mean we don't think about it; death holds a certain fascination. Most people see it as a deep mystery, an experience that they want to know more about. That fascination explains the phenomenal success of books written by people who have had near-death experiences. We want to penetrate the veil and get a glimpse of what lies beyond.

Almost everyone agrees that death is inevitable, that it's a fascinating mystery and that it's a terrifying prospect. Even the biblical writers trembled at "the terrors of death" (Psalm 55:4) and "the valley of the shadow of death" (Psalm 23:4). When they face death, some people are "completely swept away by terrors" (Psalm 73:19). No matter what other horrors of life we endure, it seems we must still face death, what the apostle Paul described as "the last enemy" (1 Corinthians 15:25-26).

Many who refuse to accept the salvation that Christ offers view death as the end of everything that is good. If you believe that death is simply the end of existence, your philosophy becomes "Go for all the gusto you can get!" God intends the shock and fear of death to bring people to repentance, but instead people seek to block the terror out with the "eating of meat and drinking of wine" (Isaiah 22:13). Many people also believe that death brings the end of pain or suffering. The philosophy behind the movement to allow physician-assisted suicide is that it is an act of mercy to bring death to a suffering human being.

To the person who refuses to believe what the Bible says about death, physical death is an impenetrable mystery. There is simply no explanation for why death comes or why it strikes or when it strikes. From the perspective of our observation alone, we are forced to conclude that everyone simply has "a time to die" (Ecclesiastes 3:2). Death seems to be a random, final, essentially meaningless end to human life. Only when we come to the Scriptures do we begin to find the important questions about death answered with certainty. The Bible doesn't answer all the questions our minds can raise about death, but the essential information is unmistakably clear.

The Dim Light of the Old Testament

Men and women who believed in the one true God before the coming of Christ had only a faint light into the experience of death. In general death was a gloomy, dreadful experience. The ancient sufferer Job felt this way toward death:

Are not my few days almost over?
Turn away from me so I can have a moment's joy
before I go to the place of no return,
to the land of gloom and deep shadow,
to the land of deepest night,
of deep shadow and disorder,
where even the light is like darkness. (Job 10:20-22)

Job's suffering prompted Job and his friends to think deeply about life and death. They used vivid images to picture the dismal end of human life on earth. Job described his life as that of a weary worker waiting for his meager pay (Job 7:1-3). As he looked back on the years of his existence, Job felt that they had passed as swiftly as a weaver's shuttle and would end without hope (7:6). From the perspective of Job's ash heap, a man's life is a flower that quickly fades, a fleeting shadow that does not endure and water that evaporates under the summer sun (14:2, 11-12). If a tree is cut down, new growth can come from the stump, but when a man dies, says Job, "he breathes his last and is no more" (14:8-10). We need to read these passages, of course, not as declarations of what is actually the case but as true reflections of a man in despair.

Bildad, one of Job's counselors, describes death in images of a lamp that is snuffed out, a pilgrim trapped and destroyed, an enemy in pursuit and a tree uprooted (18:5-17).

The Preacher of Ecclesiastes has given us one of the greatest poetic descriptions of aging and death found in literature (12:1-7). He compares the human body to a house and the aging process to the inevitable deterioration of the structure:

the arms and hands shake, the back bends, the teeth decay and fall out, hearing and eyesight fail, strength and appetite diminish, and ultimately the "pitcher is shattered at the spring" (12:6).

The uncertainty and fear of death put Old Testament believers under bondage all their lives (Hebrews 2:15). So many of God's promises to Israel were linked to the land and to material blessings that it was hard for them to envision a pleasant life beyond the material, earthly realm. Another factor that weighed on their consciences was an awareness of their own sin, which was aroused by the law of God but never fully relieved by animal sacrifices (Hebrews 10:1-4).

Old Testament believers did have some insight from God into the gloom of death. Job believed that his "Redeemer" was living. He also knew that, even though his own body would decay after death, he would experience a future resurrection and would see his Redeemer-God with his own eyes (Job 19:25-27).

The Bright Light of the Resurrection

The gloom and despair surrounding death were removed only when someone walked into the jaws of death, disarmed it of its power and returned to tell us about his victory. Jesus did exactly that! He tasted death for all humanity (Hebrews 2:9), and he conquered death through his resurrection.

When we think about Jesus' death on the cross, we usually focus on the fact that his death atoned for our sins. He suffered the full outpouring of God's holy wrath in our place. He took our penalty, and by faith in him we receive his life. Christ's death in our place is one of the central themes of the New Testament. But Jesus also died as a human being. The God-man experienced physical death! His physical death was verified by his executioners, his enemies and his closest friends. Joseph of Arimathea, Nicodemus and a few coura-geous women took a corpse down from the cross and placed it in a tomb.

The amazing declaration of the New Testament is not sim-ply that Jesus died. Men died on Roman crosses all the time. This man, however, rose again. Jesus walked into that dismal valley of death and came back to life again. He didn't return to the same kind of life he'd had before. Instead he arose to a whole new kind of life—resurrection life. By his resurrec-tion, Jesus robbed death of its grip of fear over us. In addition, Jesus beamed a clear, bright light into the darkness beyond death and let us see what awaits us there. When the apostle John saw the resurrected, glorified Lord Jesus in Revelation 1, Jesus exclaimed: "I am the Living One; I was dead, and behold I am alive for ever and ever! And I hold the keys of death and Hades" (v. 18). In Jesus' possession are the keys that unlock the fear and despair of death. Jesus as a man and as our Redeemer has conquered death forever.

The Clear Light of Faith

The fact of Jesus' victory over death should be enough to encourage us as we think about death, but the Lord has gone beyond that in order to remove the fear of death from our hearts. Throughout the New Testament we find several met-aphors or word-pictures that describe what death will be like for the Christian. Each image is designed to bring comfort, assurance and peace to our hearts as we face the deaths of people we love and as we think about our own. If the terrors of death have filled your heart, begin to replace those fearful images with God's pictures of what death will involve.

The Bible most often pictures death as *sleep* (2 Chronicles 9:31; Psalm 13:3; Daniel 12:2; John 11:11-13; 1 Corinthians 11:30; 15:51). Sleep, like death, is temporary and ends in a great awakening. When the spirit departs, the body sleeps in the dust, waiting for the resurrection. I think the image of sleep is used so often in Scripture because sleep and death are both universal experiences. From infancy to old age, human beings need sleep. When we are tired, we look forward to lying down and letting refreshing sleep sweep over us. We don't fear sleep; we welcome it, and we look forward with anticipation to a new day. For the Christian, death is falling asleep to all we have known in this realm and waking up in Christ's presence.

Jesus described his death as *an exodus* (Luke 9:31), and Peter applied the same metaphor to his own coming death (2 Peter 1:14-15). The primary reference of the word *exodus* is, of course, to the people of Israel leaving their slavery in Egypt. Their exodus was an experience of joyful release and of fearful anxiety. Death is a cruel master that would like to reign over us and hold us in its power (Romans 5:14, 21), but Christ died to free us. The writer of Hebrews says, "[Jesus] shared in their humanity so that by his death he might . . . free those who all their lives were held in slavery by their fear of death" (2:14-15). Our death is not a descent into darkness but a victorious release.

Death is also like *taking down a tent*. Our present bodies are our temporary dwelling places. The apostle Paul calls the body "the earthly tent we live in" (2 Corinthians 5:1). He adds later, "While we are in this tent, we groan and are burdened" (5:4). Our bodies are subject to weariness and disease, to pain and paralysis. When you add to that the power of sin that resides in these bodies, the despair becomes almost unbearable at times. But the assurance of the Christian is that when this earthly tent is destroyed, "we have a building from God, an eternal house in heaven, not built by human hands" (2 Corinthians 5:1). Death is the first step in the wonderful process that will bring us to a permanent, glorified body that will never age or decay or require a wheelchair.

Perhaps the most comforting New Testament image of death is that of *coming home.* In most people's minds, home represents a place of rest and security and acceptance. The biblical writers looked at heaven that way. Paul in 2 Corinthians 5:6-8 describes two places where the believer in Christ is at home. First, we can be at home "in the body," that is, in this earthly realm. While we are at home here, however, we are "away from the Lord." As much as Paul loved life and the people to whom he ministered, he longed to be in the second place called home: "[I] would prefer to be away from the body and at home with the Lord." When we are absent from the body, when our spirit separates from our body in death, we find ourselves "at home" with the Lord. For the Christian, home is a place we've never been—in the presence of Christ.

In a letter to the Philippian Christians the apostle Paul again describes death, this time picturing it as a *departure:*

If I am to go on living in the body, this will mean fruitful labor for me. Yet what shall I choose? I do not know! I am torn between the two: I desire to depart and be with Christ, which is better by far; but it is more necessary for you that I remain in the body. (Philippians 1:22-24)

The word *depart* was used of a ship loosened from its moorings to sail away from the dock. The "mooring" holding Paul to this earthly realm was his dedication to the work God had given him. But tugging at his heart was a deep desire to pull up anchor, untie the ropes and sail away. Writing to Timothy, Paul used the same image at the end of his life when he knew death was near: "The time of my departure is at hand" (2 Timothy 4:6 KJV). Paul's departure, however, was not to an unknown destination. He would depart and be with Christ. The phrase Paul uses implies a conscious, intimate, face-to-face fellowship with Christ. Paul wasn't going to sleep in death. His body would sleep, but *he* would be with Christ.

The Assuring Light of God's Promises

The comforting pictures the Bible paints of death are backed up by the solid promises of God. The world outside of Christ may tremble at the prospect of dying, but those who are Christians have the anchor of God's Word holding us secure.

First, for the Christian, death is no longer feared. In Romans chapter 8 the apostle Paul makes a list of all the things that we think might separate us from Christ. The first item on his list is death: "For I am convinced that neither *death* nor life, neither angels nor demons, neither the present nor the future, nor any powers, neither height nor depth, nor anything else in all creation, will be able to separate us from the love of God that is in Christ Jesus our Lord" (vv. 38-39). Nothing will be able to separate us from God's love—not even death! God won't lose you; he won't forget you; he won't abandon you in death. God confirms this in Hebrews 13:5 when he says, "Never will I leave you; never will I forsake you." The biblical author then tells us how to respond to this promise: "So we say with confidence, 'The Lord is my helper; I will not be afraid' " (Hebrews 13:6). Death should no longer be feared because, whatever it involves, we are convinced that it will not separate us from the love of God.

The sting of death is gone too. Paul could exclaim in 1 Corinthians 15:55, "Where, O death, is your victory? Where, O death, is your sting?" The ability of death to inflict permanent pain was removed by Jesus' victory over death. It can't terrorize us anymore. Death for us is falling asleep in Jesus; it's setting sail to a place called home.

Death is robbed of its power and pain, and of its uncertainty. Jesus has walked the dark valley ahead of us, beaming the bright light of truth along the path. In our humanity we may still tremble at death's door, but in our hearts and minds we know that this final enemy is a defeated enemy. When we find ourselves absent from the body, we will be consciously at home with the Lord.

The final (and best) promise about death that God gives us is that for a Christian death is not inevitable. The Bible is clear that there will be one generation of Christians who will not experience physical death. Christ will return someday, and we who are alive when he returns will be caught up to be with Christ forever (1 Thessalonians 4:15-17). We won't die; we will be transformed. "We will not all sleep [in death], but we will all be changed—in a flash, in the twinkling of an eye, at the last trumpet" (1 Corinthians 15:51-52). My great hope as a believer is that I won't have to die. I'd like to be alive when Christ returns. The apostle John shared that hope; he expected to still be alive when Christ returned. He said, "We know that when [Christ] appears, *we* shall be like him, for *we* shall see him as he is" (1 John 3:2).

When talking about death, I've heard a lot of people say, "I just *feel* it will be this way." Somehow their *feeling* doesn't give me much comfort. Or someone might say, "I *think* when we die this will happen." And I respond, "That's what you *think*, but you might be wrong." Someone may read an account of a near-death experience and say, "That's how it will be when we die." But that kind of experience will not be enough to anchor my soul when I bury a loved one or when I face that valley myself. I want truth, not feelings or philosophy. I want promises, not predictions. When I face death, I will lay aside my speculations and cling only to Christ and to his written promises. As I listen, he will reassure me, "I will never desert you, Doug. I will never forsake you. Hold on to me, and we will walk this last road together."

I need to add that such promises are only for those who claim Jesus Christ as their Savior. If you don't know Christ, if you have never personally trusted in him, you *ought* to be terrified of death. You will face death alone, and you will face eternity separated from Christ. But the good news is you don't have to live in fear of death. God offers you eternal life today if you in faith will receive Christ as your Savior. He died on the cross for you; he rose again in victory for you. He will change you and cleanse you from sin at this moment if you will accept his grace and forgiveness.

Facing the Final Moments
I find myself in many hospital rooms and living rooms as families watch a loved one die. Sometimes they sit in silence. Sometimes they speak or whisper expressions of love into the dying person's ear. The tenderest scenes I have witnessed at a deathbed are loving spouses or children reminding a believing wife or mother or father of the promises of God to those who are his dear children. Often the words of Scripture are the last words we whisper to loved ones who lie in the darkness of death waiting for the daybreak of heaven.

The apostle Paul wrote to the Philippian Christians about his desire to depart from this life and to be with Christ. To be with the Lord, he said, was "better by far" than anything we can know or experience here (Philippians 1:23). Earlier he wrote that, for those of us in Christ, death is gain, not loss (1:21). Don't ever wish a believer back who has gone to be with Christ. We miss them deeply, but they are in a place that is better by far. As a dear friend of mine said when her husband died, "Everyone who goes before us just makes us long all the more for heaven."

Ken Gire, in his book *Instructive Moments with the Savior*, gives a description of death that I have used often to encourage those who are dying and comfort those left behind.

Death. It is the most misunderstood part of life. It is not a great sleep but a great awakening. It is that moment when we awake, rub our eyes, and see things at last the way God has seen them all along.[1]

Chapter 2

WHY DO WE HAVE TO DIE?

*S*everal years ago I was late for an appointment with my dentist. As I sat down in his chair, I apologized for being late and explained that I had been at the hospital talking and praying with a man who in a few hours or days would die.

The dentist visibly shuddered and said, "I could never do what you do. I could never deal with dying people."

My response was immediate: "You do it every day! All of us are dying. Some of us are just further from it than others."

Death is a very real part of life. Because death touches us all, the Bible has a lot to say about it. The biblical writers, however, do not cover up the subject with whispers and flowers and organ music. The Bible speaks openly and realistically about it—and so should we. We don't approach this matter of death as do morticians or medical students who can keep a mental distance. We approach it as human beings who in the next one hundred years will all likely experience it firsthand. So we seek reliable information for our minds and positive assurance for our hearts.

The word *death* is used in the Bible to describe three different conditions or experiences. The central idea in each case is *separation*. Death in any of its forms involves a separation.

The Bible describes the first condition as *spiritual death*—the separation of a person from a relationship with God. Spiritual death is the present condition of everyone who has not believed in the Lord Jesus. Every human being at one time was dead toward God, that is, unresponsive to God's will, enslaved by sin, with a conscience deaf to God's voice. The apostle Paul made that fact very clear: "As for you, you were *dead* in your transgressions and sins, in which you used to live" (Ephesians 2:1).

That's why we need to be born again by faith in Jesus Christ. Spiritually dead people need new life.

The word *death* is also used in the Bible to describe *physical death*—the separation of the human body from the human spirit. James says, "The body without the spirit is dead" (James 2:26). I don't want to get into a long debate about whether a human being is made up of two parts (body and spirit) or three parts (body, soul and spirit). For the sake of our study in this book, we will use the perspective of James. Human beings have a material, physical part called the body and an immaterial, nonphysical part called the spirit. At death the body and the spirit are separated. Without the life of the spirit, the body dies and decays.

The third condition described in the Bible as death is the *second death*—the final and permanent separation of an unbeliever from God, sometimes called *eternal death*. The apostle John caught a glimpse of this eternal spiritual death in Revelation 20:14—"Death and Hades were thrown into the lake of fire. The lake of fire is the second death."

The remedy for spiritual death is eternal life through Jesus Christ here and now. The remedy for physical death is the resurrection, when the body and the spirit are reunited and glorified. For the second death there is no remedy.

The Root of the Problem: Why We Die

In 1994 Sherwin Nuland, a surgeon and medical-school professor, wrote a book called *How We Die.*[1] The book is an account of how various diseases like AIDS, cancer and heart disease take away human life. Nuland graphically details the causes of death.

Though not a medical textbook, the Bible deals with the causes of death too. Every death has its own story, and there are at least three causes for every physical death.

First there is the immediate cause, which can be any of an infinite number of things—a heart attack, stroke, cancer, drowning, an auto accident or whatever. The immediate cause of death is what we read in the newspaper when a death is reported.

A second factor involved in physical death is the moral cause of death. When our parents, Adam and Eve, disobeyed God's command in the Garden of Eden, one of the consequences was death. "You will surely die," God had warned (Genesis 2:17)—and they did. Spiritual death was immediate; Adam and Eve became sinners. They became aware of good and evil, but only from the perspective of evil. When they were expelled from the Garden, they were separated from intimate fellowship with God (Genesis 3:24).

While Adam and Eve did not immediately die a physical death, they did begin the process of deterioration that leads to death. The good universe that God had created became enshrouded in a curse. Sickness, pain, suffering, disease and despair now became part of the human condition. Paul in Romans 5:12 spells out the moral consequences of Adam's sin in graphic terms: "Sin entered the world through one man, and death through sin, and in this way death came to all men, because all sinned."

The immediate causes of death—sickness, deformity, deterioration, human violence and cruelty—all relate back to the entrance of sin into the human heart. Sin entered the world, and galloping in on sin's coattails was death (James 1:15). If you've ever wondered why babies starve to death or suffer cruel abuse or why at times the best of people experience the harshest deaths, these sad situations all occur as the consequences of living in a fallen, sin-cursed, sin-filled world.

Beyond the immediate and moral causes of death stands the ultimate cause of death. The one who bears final responsibility for death is God (Job 34:14-15; Acts 17:28). "The LORD brings death and makes alive; he brings down to the grave and raises up" (1 Samuel 2:6).

Our God is not unconcerned with our circumstances or powerless to help us. Nothing happens in history or in our lives that God does not directly cause or permit. Our every breath rests in his sovereign control.

A Look Behind the Scenes

I want you to see how these three causes of death are woven together in two biblical examples. First Chronicles 10 tells the poignant story of King Saul's death.

> Now the Philistines fought against Israel. . . . The fighting grew fierce around Saul, and when the archers overtook him, they wounded him. Saul said to his armor-bearer, "Draw your sword and run me through, or these uncircumcised fellows will come and abuse me." But his armor-

bearer was terrified and would not do it; so Saul took his own sword and fell on it. (vv. 1, 3-4)

The immediate causes of Saul's death are obvious—the enemy's arrows and his own sword. But later in the same passage the biblical historian gives us another insight into his death: "Saul died because he was unfaithful to the LORD; he did not keep the word of the LORD and even consulted a medium for guidance, and did not inquire of the LORD" (vv. 13-14). Saul died not only because physical death is one of the consequences of being a fallen creature, but more directly because he himself had sinned.

Finally, standing as Lord over all, God emerges as the ultimate cause of Saul's death. "So *the LORD* put [Saul] to death and turned the kingdom over to David son of Jesse" (1 Chronicles 10:14). In the shadows of human history, a sovereign God works to accomplish what he desires.

We see the same combination of causes in the Exodus account of the final plague that swept over Egypt. God had hammered away at Pharaoh's hardened heart, but he still refused to let the people of Israel go free. Finally God brought a judgment that moved even Pharaoh. He allowed the "destroyer" to kill the first-born child of every Egyptian family. To protect the Israelite children, Moses obeyed God's instructions and told the people to rub the blood of a sacrificed lamb on the doorframes of their houses: "When the LORD goes through the land to strike down the Egyptians, he will see the blood . . . and will pass over that doorway, and he will not permit the destroyer to enter your houses and strike you down" (Exodus 12:23).

The "destroyer" was most likely Satan—the one who held the power of death (see Hebrews 2:14). The immediate cause of the death of every first-born child was the attack of the destroyer. The moral cause was the stubborn refusal of the

Egyptians to obey the command of God. But ultimately God bears the responsibility for what happened that dreadful night in Egypt: "At midnight *the* LORD struck down all the firstborn in Egypt" (Exodus 12:29).

Every death, including yours and mine, will tell its own story. The immediate cause will most likely be something tragic—a destructive disease, a horrible accident, a violent assault or even the inevitable deterioration of age. That's the cause people will talk about.

But behind that immediate cause will stand a greater force, the steady decline produced by sin's devastating power. Perhaps our own personal sin will contribute to our death. Alcohol, smoking and overeating can all contribute to our decline.

To some Christians, death may come as the severe chastening of God. In Paul's letter to the Corinthian church, he warned them of their abuse of the Lord's Supper or the Communion service. Some who continued to receive the Lord's Supper with an attitude of disrespect had become weak or sick, and some were dead (1 Corinthians 11:30). James, as he writes about anointing the sick, warns us that some sickness is the result of unconfessed sin. Our response should be to confess our sins to each other that we might be healed (James 5:13-16).

Please do not misinterpret what I've said. Not all sickness or death is God's chastening, but it can be. I've attended some funerals that I believed were the evidence of God's holy hand of judgment in the life of a Christian who refused to repent.

Mercifully, God has not abandoned us to suffer the inevitable consequences of sin. He is in control of all the events of our lives. The apostle Paul believed that the reason the Lord had not taken him to heaven by death was that there was still work for Paul to do (Philippians 1:22-26). But once the fight had been fought and the race had been won, Paul knew his promotion to glory would not be long in coming.

In May of 1993 one of the elders in our church died. He was forty-two years old. He left a beautiful wife and two teen-age daughters, as well as a brother, and parents, and lots of friends, who all had one question: why? The doctors said the immediate cause was a massive heart attack. The theologians among us tried to explain that in a sinful, fallen world like ours, sometimes young men die. Neither of those explana-tions brought much comfort to a grieving family. The only rock of assurance we could hold on to in those days was that the God we love and trust is a God of purpose. For his own reasons, which we may never see or understand in this life, he allowed a forty-two-year-old father to die.

In the darkest nights of our pain and loss, all we can hold on to is the Lord we love—and to our amazement we find in those difficult days that it is actually the Father we love who holds on to us.

Chapter 3

THE LIE AT THE END OF THE TUNNEL

Near-Death Experiences

*T*he *most compelling accounts of what happens after death come* from people who have had near-death or after-death experiences and then have returned to write bestselling books. The popular fascination with such experiences began in 1975 when a medical doctor, Raymond Moody, wrote a book called *Life After Life*. In that book and its sequel, *Reflections on Life After Life*, Moody related the experiences of several patients who had come close to death. Since then people have flooded the bookshelves and television talk shows with dramatic accounts of their experiences after clinical death.

The most detailed account of an after-death experience has come from Betty Eadie in the book *Embraced by the Light*.

Eadie claims that in November 1973 she was "dead" for more than four hours. During that time her spirit was transported to heaven, where she was embraced by Jesus Christ and was given a tour. Finally, in front of a council of twelve men, Eadie was told that her work on earth was not done and that she would have to return. Reluctantly, and after extracting a promise from the heavenly council that as soon as her work was done she would be allowed to return, she agreed to come back to earth. Part of Betty Eadie's mission apparently was to tell her story. Since its publication in 1992, the book has sold well over two million copies and has appeared on every best-seller list.

I learned about Betty Eadie's story when a friend thrust a copy into my hands and said, "You *have* to read this book!" I did read it—and I was deeply disturbed by what I read. I was disturbed by the departure of Eadie's experience from the clear declarations of Scripture about what happens after we die.[1] When I returned the book to my friend, I didn't give it a very positive evaluation. I told him that Eadie's experience did not harmonize with biblical truth at all. It was drawn instead from the teachings of Mormonism and the writings of the Mormon founder, Joseph Smith. For example, Eadie repeatedly talks about her "pre-mortal" existence and her "memory" of people and events before her earthly life. She even "remembered" the creation of the earth.[2] This premortal existence is a foundational part of Mormon theology. According to Mormonism, the God of this planet, Elohim, and his celestial wife (or wives) by sexual union produced billions of spirit children, who lived in heaven before coming to earth to begin their own journey toward godhood. I told my friend that if Eadie's teaching on the afterlife was true, the Bible's teaching is wrong.

My friend was upset—not because the book promoted

Mormon teaching but because I was unwilling to accept it as an accurate portrayal of what follows death. He said, "Here is a woman who has been through death and who has come back to tell us about it, and you won't listen!"

That's the problem with making evaluations. People think you are being judgmental and harsh. In an interview with a journalist about my evaluation of Eadie's book, the journalist was very unhappy with my criticism of a book he personally had enjoyed and had recommended to several other people. He ended the interview by saying, "I don't think we should judge other people like you have done. I think we should just affirm everyone's experience and try to learn something good from it."

His remark sounds noble. The problem is that we as Christians *are* responsible to judge what we hear and read and see. We are commanded to evaluate our own experiences and others' as well against the measuring stick of God's Word. The apostle John exhorted us to "test the spirits" in our world (1 John 4:1-3). Jesus had no hesitation about exposing wrong thinking or unbiblical belief in his society. We certainly are not to be judgmental in a self-righteous or hypocritical way, but we are to carefully evaluate the teaching of those who claim to give us spiritual insight. In the same sermon where Jesus said, "Do not judge, or you too will be judged," he also said, "Watch out for false prophets" (Matthew 7:1, 15). Jesus concluded by saying that the standard we are to use in evaluating both the words and actions of those who claim to give spiritual direction is "these words of mine" (Matthew 7:21-24). If a person's experience or teaching is in harmony with what God has said in his Word, we can accept it. If what we are told is not in harmony with Scripture, even if it comes from an angel from heaven, we are to reject it (Galatians 1:8-9).

Are Near-Death Experiences Genuine?

My own study of the Bible's teaching on death and on life after death and my reading of the experiences of those who claim to have had near-death encounters have made me skeptical of near-death claims. As you will see, I'm not a total skeptic, but I am pretty hard to convince. I'm not questioning the person's honesty or even that he or she really had the experience they tell about. What I question is whether the experience is an accurate reflection of what death will be like.

The first problem that near-death or after-death experiences raise in my mind is, Did the person really die? Medical science defines death as the absence of vital signs (heartbeat, respiration, reflex) or the absence of brain-wave activity. The Bible defines death as the separation of the spirit from the body (James 2:26). Many of the characteristic features of near-death experiences (the sense of leaving one's body, movement through a dark tunnel toward a bright light, a sense of warmth and peace, seeing one's life in review) have been linked to a loss of oxygen or even to certain brain functions brought on by the stress or trauma of a physical emergency.[3]

Medically we have no way of knowing when the spirit leaves the body. So we can't really say when death occurs. Lack of heartbeat or respiration may *normally* indicate physical death, but it may not *always* indicate genuine death. My opinion is that some of the people who have had near-death experiences simply experienced the body's reaction to serious trauma.

Another difficulty I have from a biblical viewpoint is the declaration of Hebrews 9:27 that a person dies *once*. I realize that there have been some notable exceptions to that statement. When Jesus raised Lazarus to life, Lazarus returned to the same kind of life he had known before (John 11:38-44). At some point Lazarus died physically a second time. That was true of every person in history who was raised from the dead by God's miraculous power. But if you add up every "revival" of a person who had died that is recorded in the Bible, only fifteen or twenty have had that experience in all of history. It seems difficult to believe that, suddenly in the last few decades, God is bringing hundreds of people through death and then back to life again.

I certainly do not have a complete explanation for every near-death experience, nor am I questioning the integrity of those who tell their stories. I do believe, however, that we need to be gently skeptical of the accounts we hear. Such individual experiences do not prove anything about the afterlife.

Personally I am convinced that much of what we hear regarding such encounters is our enemy's deliberate attempt to deceive people about what really lies beyond death's door. The prospect of death and of personal accountability to God has often moved people to seriously consider the claims of Christ and their own destinies. If people believe, however, based on a few near-death encounters, that death will lead them to a place of warmth and love and acceptance regardless of their relationship to Christ, they will no longer be moved to evaluate their lives. Satan will have masked their fear of death and removed another element that might have brought them to repentance. The attraction of the saving power of Christ fades if a person is deceived into thinking that he or she does not need saving.

That is why I emphasize the importance of lovingly pointing the people we know to the truth of the Bible. Our confidence has to rest on God's Word. Jesus Christ is declared in the Bible to be God the Son, God in human flesh. Jesus, therefore, is a fully trustworthy witness who *has* died and who *has* returned from the clutches of death and the grave. Jesus' story may not seem as enthralling as the latest bestselling book, but we can trust it totally as an accurate, fully reliable account of what awaits us beyond death's door.

Visions Beyond Death

Just so you won't think I'm a total skeptic, let me balance the first part of this chapter with biblical accounts of some people who came near death or who saw beyond death. Oddly enough, none of the people who died and then was revived miraculously to life says one recorded word about the experience of death. Lazarus never tells us what it was like to be dead four days and then called forth by the Lord Jesus. But a few people as they died were given insights into the heavenly realm and spoke some words of comfort and assurance.

Stephen, a deacon in the Jerusalem church, gave a masterful defense of the faith before the Jewish council in Acts 7. As these councilmen were convicted in their hearts of the truth of Stephen's message, their anger sparked, and they rushed up to kill him. At that moment, Stephen gazed into heaven and saw God's glorious presence and Jesus standing at the Father's right hand. Over the council's shouts of anger, Stephen's voice rose. " 'Look,' he said, 'I see heaven open and the Son of Man standing at the right hand of God' " (Acts 7:56).

The most extended vision of life in the future was given to the apostle John in exile on the island of Patmos. He recorded what he saw and heard in the book of Revelation. In chapter 4 of the book the risen Lord Jesus says to John, "Come up here," and John saw the world's future from a heavenly perspective.

The apostle Paul had a vision of heaven too. In 2 Corinthians 12 Paul tells us that a man was "caught up to paradise"—a man most Bible students believe was Paul himself.

I know a man in Christ who fourteen years ago was caught up to the third heaven. Whether it was in the body or out of the body I do not know—God knows. And I know that this man—whether in the body or apart from the body I do not know, but God knows—was caught up to paradise. He heard inexpressible things, things that man is not permitted to tell. (2 Corinthians 12:2-4)

I think it is worth noting that John wrote a whole book about his vision, but Paul says that he was restrained from telling what he saw and heard. God even allowed a thorn in the flesh—probably some physical ailment—to afflict Paul; it was designed, Paul says, "to harass me, to keep me from being too elated" (2 Corinthians 12:7 RSV). So Paul was not given the privilege of boasting in his vision. He had to be content with his own memory of it, and he had to contend with a painful affliction because of it.

Someone might raise the same objection to these biblical experiences that I raised to the near-death experiences we hear about today. They might say, "These individual experiences don't *prove* anything about what lies beyond death for the rest of us." But there are two major differences between what Paul and John describe and what most near-death experiences of our day claim. First, the experiences of John, Paul and Stephen are recorded in Scripture with the implication that what they saw was the truth and, to a degree, normative for every believer. We may not be given a vision of Jesus before or as we die, but we will be ushered directly into his presence at death. I think it's powerfully significant that while the writer of Hebrews pictures Jesus as *seated* at the Father's right hand (Hebrews 8:1), Stephen saw Jesus standing. Jesus stands up to welcome his child into his heavenly home. The second difference between the biblical accounts and present-day near-death experiences is that each biblical account harmonizes with what we are told in other passages of Scripture about death and the afterlife. Most contemporary accounts of near-death experiences stand in direct contradiction to the Bible's teaching.

"I Saw the City"

I've known three people who have had predeath visions of heaven. The first was a man who could only be described as the patriarch of the church I pastored. He was small and thin, but when he got up to speak in a meeting a hush fell over everyone. We all knew that what George Strickland had to say would be important and insightful. One Sunday evening as I was about to preach, an usher handed me a note that Mr. Strickland had been taken that afternoon to the hospital. At the close of the service I went immediately to his bedside. He seemed asleep, but when I spoke his name his eyes opened. He said, "What are you doing here?" I replied, "What are *you* doing here?" In a quiet voice he said, "I won't be here much longer. This afternoon I had a dream, and I saw a magnificent city far away. When I woke up, I knew in my heart from the Lord that I'm headed for that city." Within twenty-four hours Mr. Strickland had died.

Berniece Mohr had emphysema and pneumonia. Every breath was a struggle, and the doctors told her family that she would not survive the night. I prayed at her bed and went home. The next morning I went back to the hospital, and she was still alive. As I walked into her room, I said, "I didn't expect to see you still here this morning." She responded, "I didn't expect you would either!" After a few moments of silence she added, "Last night I saw the lights." "The lights?" I asked. Her answer was spoken in awe. "The lights of the city. Spread out before me but far away—a wonderful city." Berniece lived two more years after that encounter with death. Last year she made another trip to that city to stay.

The third person I have known who has seen heaven is still

alive. Registering no heartbeat or blood pressure, Ione Turcott was taken to the hospital. The doctors and nurses worked on her for a long time with almost no response. At the urging of a nurse who knew Ione they worked even longer than they normally would have, and finally her heart stabilized. Ione's husband, Don, was in the waiting room, and a nurse went to get him. As he entered the room, Ione's eyes were open, and she was smiling. As she began to talk, Don said, "She's been there! She's been to heaven!" Ione doesn't remember everything she saw and heard. Some of it was blocked from her memory. But she is convinced that God in his grace gave her a vision of heaven's glory to encourage her own heart and to bless those who hear her story.

I've never had a vision of heaven, and I suspect that most Christians won't before they die. Only a few of the saints whose deaths are recorded in Scripture saw through the veil of death. If we don't have a vision, that's not a sign that God loves us less than those who have. It simply shows that God for his own good purposes may choose to give an extra measure of assurance to a believer who needs it. But God has given all of us his precious promises, and a promise from God is more secure than any vision or anyone's personal experience. What has sustained most of the believers I have known in the final hours of life is not visions or the experiences of others but the knowledge that they are held in the unfailing arms of God.

Chapter 4

REINCARNATION, ANNIHILATION & OTHER VIEWS

*N*ot everyone agrees on what happens to us after we die. If you ask ten coworkers or buddies at the gym what they think happens after death, you will probably get eleven different opinions.

The wide variety of opinion on life after death was pressed home to me several months ago as I sat in a graduate class called "Contemporary Religious Movements." The guest speaker was a member of a religious group that believes in reincarnation. They also believe that each person can remember his or her past lives. The woman addressing the class had been a male commander in Joshua's army. (She also told us that the biblical Joshua was really a previous life embodiment of Jesus!) She also had been a Jew who was killed in the Roman destruction of Jerusalem in A.D. 70. She had, in fact, lived thousands of lives. She even claimed to have discovered one that very week. In the course of a massage, she had felt a pain in her neck. As her therapist massaged the area, the woman suddenly remembered that she had been a medieval Waldensian girl who had been dragged by the neck to be burned at the stake by Catholic inquisitors!

Popular views, like this, of what happens after we die may be fascinating and incredible, but the real measure of their truthfulness is how well they agree with what the Bible says. Part of holding a consistent Christian view of death involves knowing the truth as God has revealed it. But that is not enough. We must also reject views that depart from clear biblical teaching and actively defend biblical truth against views that disagree with it.

Standing for the truth of Scripture is not a popular position in our culture. The emerging relativistic consensus is that everyone is entitled to his or her own religious views and that no view can be declared right or wrong. I'm certainly an advocate of religious freedom; I'm an equally strong advocate of the need for Christians to stand courageously in a culture without spiritual foundations and to say, "This is what God clearly says." We've allowed "cultural correctness" to pressure us into silence. Jesus certainly had no problem exposing the faulty religious views of people in his day, and we should be just as courageous in defending the truth of Scripture today— both inside and outside the church. Our faith is based on what God has declared in his Son and in his Word, not on the most recent breeze to blow across our society.

What people facing death need are the clear, unshakable promises of God, not the weak, hope-so opinions of the latest guru. The most loving thing you can do for the neighbor or coworker or fellow student who has embraced a false view of death or Christ or salvation is to share the truth of the gospel and the Scriptures with them. If Jesus is the truth that he claimed to be, then we are called to be lights shining in a very dark place.

Reincarnation

The belief that human beings are reborn to earthly existence after death is not new. The concept of reincarnation first appeared in early Hindu writings about 1000 B.C. Every religion derived from Hinduism, including classical Buddhism, has accepted some variation of belief in reincarnation. For centuries it has been the belief of the majority of the human race; in the last twenty years it has become accepted in some form by more than one-fourth of all Americans.[1] The original view of reincarnation was based on the belief in the transmigration of the soul, which holds that the soul can be embodied in plants and animals as well as in humans. Western versions of reincarnation have limited the cycle of rebirth to human forms only.

Closely associated with reincarnation is the concept of karma. The law of karma says that the good deeds or evil deeds in a person's past lives are reflected in that person's current life situation. The final objective of all reincarnation is to merge with the ultimate reality of the universe, variously described as nothingness, or God, or oneness with God. As a person's legacy of good deeds and self-denial builds, the person climbs higher and higher on the chain of perfection until no more embodiments are necessary. The person becomes or merges with deity.

In Western culture, reincarnation was embraced by the Greek philosophers Plato and Pythagoras, and later by Roman Stoics, Gnostics and the followers of the Greek mystery religions. The modern Western expression of reincarnation began to emerge in the eighteenth century but was popularized by the nineteenth-century occult religion of Theosophy. In the twentieth century, psychics like Edgar Cayce and Jeane Dixon were outspoken proponents of reincarnation. The contemporary New Age movement has wholeheartedly endorsed and promoted belief in reincarnation.

Biblical Christianity, on the other hand, has always rejected reincarnation—with good reason. Human beings are not progressing upward to God through an endless cycle of rebirths. Instead we are all lost, dead in our sins and separated from the life of God. What redeems us from that dreadful situation is the grace and forgiveness of God, who, because of the atoning sacrifice of Christ on the cross, is free to forgive those who come to him in faith. Furthermore, as we will see later in this book, the Bible clearly teaches that at death the soul or spirit separates from the body and goes either into Christ's presence or into a place of judgment. The final blow to belief in reincarnation is the declaration of Hebrews 9:27: "Man is destined to die *once*, and after that to face judgment."

When Jesus was being crucified, a thief on the cross next to him acknowledged his own sin and asked Jesus in faith to remember him with favor in Christ's future kingdom. Jesus did not promise this man a higher incarnation in his next life. Instead Jesus said, "Today you will be with me in paradise" (Luke 23:39-43).

Perhaps reincarnation is becoming more widely accepted in Western culture because it is convenient to believe. It is easier to think that you will return to human life again than that you will have to give an account of this life to God, who has the power to cast people into eternal separation from him. Reincarnation also appeals to human pride by teaching that a person's final destiny rests on human effort, not on the grace or judgment of God. Even human sin is not looked on as something wrong before God but rather as a learning experience, a potential step in a person's upward progress.

The woman who believed she had lived thousands of lives may have been utterly sincere in her belief, but she was sincerely wrong! Jesus was not a reincarnation of the Old Testament general Joshua, and she had not lived in the Middle Ages. The entire testimony of Jesus and the Bible stands against accepting any form of reincarnation as true.

Soul-Sleep

If you've ever had a long discussion with a Jehovah's Witness or a Seventh-day Adventist, you have probably been exposed to the concept of soul-sleep. The argument supporting this view goes like this: A human being is a unity; the body and soul (or spirit) together make a person. Therefore, if the body ceases to function, so does the soul. Those who hold this belief claim that after death the body *and* the soul sleep until the resurrection, when the full person (body and soul) is awakened to face the glory of heaven or the judgment of hell.

I recently had two Jehovah's Witnesses come to my door. One topic we discussed was our existence immediately after death. These men quoted two Scripture verses to demonstrate that the soul is asleep or unconscious after death: "For the living know that they will die, but the dead know nothing" (Ecclesiastes 9:5); and "Whatever your hand finds to do, do it with all your might, for in the grave [Sheol], where you are going, there is neither working nor planning nor knowledge nor wisdom" (Ecclesiastes 9:10).

I tried to point out that these verses are a record of what the Teacher of Ecclesiastes "observed" going on "under the sun," that is, in this earthly realm. He even admits that by observation alone we can't comprehend all that *God* does (Ecclesiastes 8:16-17). Simply from the perspective of human observation, it looks like when we die, we are totally without ability to function—no working, no planning, no knowledge. If the folks who base so much on these verses would read further in Ecclesiastes, they would find the Teacher's final conclusion as he contemplates the words given by God, the "one Shepherd" (12:11). After the Teacher describes old age and death, he says, "The dust [body] returns to the ground it came from, and the spirit returns to God who gave it" (12:7).

Some evangelical Christians have embraced a belief similar to soul-sleep. They believe that there can be no separation of the body and the soul or spirit. We are simply dead until Christ returns and resurrects us. Because we have no consciousness during that time it *seems* like we are immediately in Christ's presence when we die.

The New Testament, however, makes it clear that the spirit can exist in consciousness apart from the body. In the apostle John's vision into heaven, he saw "the *souls* of those who had been slain" under the heavenly altar. They cried out to God, understood God's reply and were consciously aware of events both in heaven and on earth (Revelation 6:9-11). The same consciousness is exhibited by the rich man and Lazarus in Jesus' story of the afterlife. It cannot describe events *after* the resurrection, because the rich man's five brothers were still on earth (Luke 16:19-31, especially vv. 27-28). So Jesus portrayed people as being consciously awake in the period between death and the resurrection. In Philippians 1:23-24 Paul makes a clear distinction between being "in the body" here on earth and being "with Christ" after death. The concept of soul-sleep seems to me to be an inadequate explanation of our existence after death.

Annihilation

The average secularist who gives little or no thought to God believes that at death we simply cease to exist. We've already seen that the Bible clearly contradicts that view. As much as secular humanists, atheists and materialists may deny it, death is not the end of human existence.

Annihilationism, however, is not a view held only by those outside the church; it's a view held more and more by men and women who claim allegiance to Christ. The basic points of belief are (1) that God alone possesses immortality, (2) that God grants immortality as a gift to those human beings who come to Christ in faith, and (3) that those outside of Christ either cease to exist or are allowed to perish gradually through the corrosive effect of evil. Annihilation of the unsaved seems to be preferable to the belief that people continue indefinitely immersed in the judgment and torment of hell. It is inconsistent with God's love, we are told, for him to allow any of his creatures to endure forever in torment.

While this view relieves our human minds of the incredible burden of contemplating eternal hell, the measure of truth is not if it makes us feel better or if it seems like a more reasonable solution to a difficult issue. The measure of truth is what God has revealed, and it is my conviction that the arguments for the annihilation of the unsaved cannot begin to overthrow the substantial testimony of scriptural evidence that those who refuse God's grace in Christ will be consigned to endless conscious suffering. We will examine the biblical evidence for the reality of hell in a later chapter, but for now it is enough to say that Jesus, the Old Testament prophets and the apostles all agreed that the person outside of Christ will be separated from the conscious presence of God forever. I think it is clear that the lost will perish, not by vanishing but by being deprived of the essential element of worthwhile existence—fellowship with the living God. I should point out, too, that those who spoke most forcefully about future punishment in the biblical record are Jesus and the apostle John, the very same men who also spoke most compellingly about the love of God.

Purgatory

The teachings of the Roman Catholic Church include belief in a place of punishment after death called purgatory. The doctrine actually developed during the Middle Ages and was cemented into dogma as a reaction to the Protestant Reformation, which rejected the idea of purgatory. The Council of Trent (1545-1563) declared that those who reject the doctrine of purgatory are accursed.

Catholic teaching says that those who die at peace with the church but who are not yet perfect must undergo purifying suffering. In the earlier centuries of this belief the Catholic church taught that purgatory was where divine justice was meted out for the sins people had committed after baptism. Because some sins are more grievous to God than others, the length of time and the degree of punishment varied with each person. The church also claimed that gifts to the church, prayers by priests and masses provided by relatives or friends in behalf of the person who had died could shorten or eliminate the punishment of purgatory. The pope had the power to grant outright absolution in certain cases. Once the sins had been purged, the believer was admitted to heaven. All unbaptized adults and those who had committed mortal sins after baptism were consigned immediately to hell.

In more recent years the atoning aspect of the suffering in purgatory has been played down. The emphasis has moved more toward the perfecting aspect of purgatory; it prepares the soul for heaven by purging out sinful or unholy traits.

The question to ask about belief in purgatory is, Does this

view of life after death harmonize with what the Bible teaches? The answer is no. Not one verse of Scripture supports a belief in purgatory. The only supportive text that the Catholic Church appeals to is a passage from the Apocrypha—2 Maccabees 12:43-45. In the context, Judas Maccabeus leads his Jewish army against an enemy army. A few of the Jewish soldiers are killed in the conflict. As Judas's troops recover the bodies of their comrades for burial, they discover that each of the dead men had concealed a small idol under his tunic. They had lost their lives for that reason. In what is portrayed as a noble gesture, Judas urges the people to take an offering to Jerusalem to have a sacrifice for sin offered. His hope is that ultimately these men will receive the recompense of the pious. The passage concludes with these words: "This is why he had this atonement sacrifice offered for the dead, so that they might be released from their sins" (2 Maccabees 12:45 Jerusalem Bible).

Two serious problems are raised by this passage. First, the book of 2 Maccabees was never included with the books recognized by the Jews as Scripture. Only the Roman Catholic Church accepts it as Scripture. But even if it were Scripture, the action of Judas Maccabeus contradicts Catholic belief. The men who were killed in the battle were guilty of idolatry, which in Catholic theology is a mortal sin. Those who commit mortal sins do not go to purgatory but to hell, and the prayers or offerings of people still on earth will never release a soul from hell.

Another biblical problem with the belief in purgatory is that it devalues the redemptive power of the cross of Christ. The writer of Hebrews declares that Jesus "is able to save *completely* those who come to God through him" (Hebrews 7:25). The apostle John adds that "the blood of Jesus, his Son, purifies us from *all* sin" (1 John 1:7). Purgatory doesn't purify; Christ's blood accomplishes for us what we could never accomplish by our own efforts. The apostle Peter writes, "Christ died for sins once for all, the righteous for the unrighteous, to bring you to God" (1 Peter 3:18). We don't have to work off our sins to get to God; Christ's death tore down that wall separating us from God the Father. As Paul practically shouts in Romans 8:1: "There is *now* no condemnation for those who are in Christ Jesus." Later he adds, "Who will bring any charge against those whom God has chosen? It is God who justifies" (8:33). No condemnation! No charge of accusation! Everything that can be laid to our account has already been paid in full by someone else, Jesus Christ.

Tony Coffey was born, baptized and raised in the Catholic Church. He came to a spiritual crossroad in his life in 1967 and decided to cling only to Christ for salvation and no longer to religious ritual. As Coffey writes about his spiritual journey, he says that purgatory was one belief he had a hard time giving up. The simple fact was that he did not feel he deserved to go to heaven without first spending time in purgatory. His own words tell the story best.

I really thought I was holding up the honor of the Lord with my defense of purgatory. But such comments betray a failure to understand what the sacrifice of Jesus really achieved. Not one of us deserves to go to heaven; we all deserve eternal punishment for our sins. But God, in his great love for us, hasn't given us what we deserve. Instead, he gave us his Son, whose death upon the cross pays the penalty for all the sin we have committed. His payment makes it possible for us to go to heaven when we die. We have God's word that this is in fact the case. Don't doubt it.[2]

Chapter 5

DEATH
BY CHOICE

Suicide &
Euthanasia

*I*n *the summer of 1992 my uncle committed suicide. He had been* a pastor and missionary; he was a husband, father and grandfather. He was in good physical condition, and he laughed easily. But on a warm June day, for reasons known only to him and to God, he chose to end his life.

I had the privilege of participating in my uncle's funeral— and I knew exactly what I wanted to say. The day my father called me to tell me what had happened, my mind was drawn to some words of the apostle Paul that I had pondered several times before. In 2 Corinthians 1, Paul describes a time when he passed through deep difficulty and hardship. He uses words like *affliction* and *suffering* and *despair* to press home the desperation he felt. His most gripping statement is in verse 8:

"We were under great pressure, far beyond our ability to endure, so that *we despaired even of life*" (2 Corinthians 1:8). Paul may have been arrested in Asia and even sentenced to death; he may have had to face the fury of a threatening mob. But I think he was speaking of something more personal. The pressures and concerns of ministry, fatigue from spiritual battle as he preached the gospel, perhaps a feeling of discouragement that seems to come at times to many of God's servants combined to make him wonder if it was really worth it to continue to live.

I concluded my part in the funeral service by reminding those who had gathered that the impact of my uncle's life was to be measured by his years of devotion to Christ, not by how his life had ended. My intention was not to minimize the tragedy of suicide. That decision has left some deep scars in the lives of those left behind, but it is not the full story of a man's life either.

A Fatal Mistake

Seven suicides are recorded in the Bible, and they all are portrayed as tragic, desperate events. The first recorded suicide was of Abimelech, the son of Gideon. Abimelech ordered his armor-bearer to kill him after he had been fatally wounded by a millstone that was dropped on his head (Judges 9:54). A later judge of Israel, Samson, brought down a building, killing himself and hundreds of Philistines (Judges 16:26-30). Israel's first king, Saul, fell on his own sword after being mortally wounded in battle (1 Samuel 31:4). Saul's armor-bearer refused Saul's request to kill the king but killed himself as Saul had done (1 Samuel 31:5). Ahithophel, a traitor to King David, hanged himself when David's rebellious son, Absalom, rejected his advice (2 Samuel 17:23). An evil king of Israel, Zimri, set the palace on fire and died after only seven days of rule (1 Kings 16:18). The most notorious biblical suicide was the one committed by Judas Iscariot after he had betrayed Jesus. He threw the betrayal money into the temple and then hanged himself (Matthew 27:5).

None of these accounts explicitly condemns suicide as a crime or a sin, but throughout the history of the church, suicide has never been regarded as an act that pleases God. The most influential text has been the sixth commandment: "You shall not murder" (Exodus 20:13; Deuteronomy 5:17; Matthew 19:18; Romans 13:9). Since suicide is self-murder, it is an act that clearly violates God's command. The early church theologians consistently condemned suicide and even cautioned Christians who had an active desire for martyrdom. Augustine saw suicide as an act of cowardice.

The Christian view of suicide contrasts dramatically with the view being adopted by a larger and larger segment of our society that suicide is a heroic act. When a rock singer or film star decides to "check out" or "trip out" fatally, that person is revered as someone who has committed the ultimate sacrifice or who has registered the grand protest against a meaningless existence. More and more young people find suicide a compelling end to a life they feel is empty or aimless.

I am not a psychologist or counselor, but I have explored this subject of suicide enough to know that we should take it very seriously. If you are thinking about suicide or have mentally thought of a plan for taking your own life, you need to talk to someone who will listen and who will help you. Please don't swear that person to secrecy. They need to be able to link you to someone who is equipped to help you find your way out of your despair or anger. If the person you go to first brushes it off or won't listen, keep talking—or shouting—until someone takes you seriously. A parent or pastor or friend is a good place to start. The Lord *can* deliver you from that "sentence of death," but you have to be willing to begin the process (see 2 Corinthians 1:9-11).

If you have a friend or child who mentions suicide even casually, don't take it casually. Eight out of ten people who commit suicide talk about it or exhibit warning signs (like giving away possessions) before they actually commit the act. Listen to the person; be courageous enough to pursue any hints or comments. It's better to be annoying than to live with regret afterward.

The most powerful essay I have ever read about suicide was written by Anne-Grace Scheinin in 1983. Scheinin had wrestled with thoughts of suicide for several years and twice had seriously attempted it. Then her own mother killed herself, and she experienced and saw the pain that the family had to bear. As a survivor, Scheinin writes haunting words— words to remember if (or when) the tempter whispers the fatal suggestion in your ears.

I'm alive because of my mother's death. She taught me that in spite of my illness I had to live. Suicide just isn't worth it.

I saw the torment my mother's death caused others: my father, my brother, her neighbors and friends. When I saw their overwhelming grief, I knew I could never do the same thing she had done—force other people to take on the burden of pain I'd leave behind if I died by my own hand.

Suicide is not a normal death. It is tragic beyond the most shattering experiences, and the ultimate form of abandonment. . . .

I will not, cannot, end my life as my mother did. Suicide no longer can offer me any peace. . . .

[My mother] taught me the most valuable lesson of my life: no matter how bad the pain is, it's never so bad that suicide is the only answer. It's never so bad that the only escape is a false one. Suicide doesn't end pain. It only lays it on the broken shoulders of the survivors.[1]

What If the Suffering Is Unbearable?

Most of us as Christians don't fear *death;* we fear what may be involved in the process of *dying.* We've seen family members or friends die long, painful deaths from disease or disability, and our thought is, *Dear God, please take me quickly when it's time for me to die.*

Several people in our culture have come forward with a "solution" to the suffering of those who are terminally ill or who have crippling, painful diseases. They advocate "physician-assisted suicide"—permission granted to medical professionals to legally administer lethal doses of medications to patients who have chosen to end their lives. Physician-assisted suicide is portrayed as humane ("it ends human suffering") and as the supreme exercise of individual liberty ("a right to die").

The issue of physician-assisted suicide is not a matter to be decided on the basis of the Constitution or even on whether it is declared to be a "legal" act. From a biblical standpoint, it is indefensible. Physician-assisted suicide is based on three unbiblical foundations.

First, advocates of the practice claim that death ends human suffering. Death certainly does end physical suffering for those who are in Christ, but as we will see in a later chapter, death will usher some people into a place of torment. Many advocates and practitioners of physician-assisted suicide, like Jack Kevorkian in Detroit, tirade angrily about "religious" arguments against the practice. They want society to take a purely secular approach to the issue and leave religious or biblical issues out of the debate.

The second foundation on which support of physician-assisted suicide rests is that death and the circumstances of death are matters that we as human beings have the right and authority to choose. But the Bible consistently proclaims that the opposite is true. Death and life are the sole prerogatives of God. Job declares: "Man's days are determined; you have decreed the number of his months and have set limits he cannot exceed" (Job 14:5). David adds, "All the days ordained for me were written in your book before one of them came to be" (Psalm 139:16).

But does God really want us to experience prolonged suffering if we are going to die anyway? The third foundation used as support of physician-assisted suicide is that it is an act of compassion to end prolonged and painful suffering. How can we ignore the pleading of those who want to die?

Several individuals in the Bible were so sick or depressed that it appeared to them (and to others) that they would die— but they didn't die. In fact, great blessing came to them after they recovered! Job is one of the most powerful biblical examples. Job lost everything—his wealth, his financial security, his family, his health. He sat on an ash heap scraping the sores that covered his body, and his wife made the fatal suggestion: "Curse God and die!" That was a clear invitation, I believe, to suicide. Job's reply exposed the essential self-centeredness of the suggestion. "You are talking like a foolish woman. Shall we accept good from God, and not trouble?" (Job 2:9-10). When Job's friends saw his condition, they held a funeral for him! They were so convinced that Job would die that they began to weep, tear their robes and throw dust on their heads (Job 2:12). Job himself wanted to die; he prayed to die; he asked to die. What if someone had said, "Job, you've suffered enough. I will release you from your pain with this fatal dose of morphine"? Job would have missed the transformation of character that suffering brings and the tremendous blessings that God poured out on him after his recovery.

The day came in the life of Elijah the prophet when he wanted to die. He was on the run from Jezebel, who wanted to kill him; he was exhausted and felt all alone. He even *prayed* to die (1 Kings 19:4). Why didn't God say, "All right, Elijah, if it's your choice to die, I will let you die"? Instead God restored Elijah's strength and perspective, and Elijah lived many more years of faithful service to God.

I certainly don't want to sound heartless or unsympathetic to people who are suffering intense physical and emotional pain. I've stood by too many bedsides and watched too many faithful Christians suffer through long months and years of pain to be unsympathetic. My wife's mother lingered through weeks of discomfort and agony as she died. We prayed that God would be merciful and take her life quickly, but his answer seemed a long time in coming. I am simply forced by my understanding of God's truth to conclude that the deliberate termination of human life is *wrong*. It is wrong because God may choose to bring healing or restoration or a time of remission to that person. It is wrong because God's purposes in that person's own life and through that person in the lives of others may not yet be accomplished. And it is wrong to terminate human life deliberately and actively because of the sanctity of all human life—born and unborn, young and old, normal and retarded, capable and incapable. Human beings are made in the image of God, and we have no right to arbitrarily take life for the sake of convenience or choice.

We as Christians need to speak out courageously in our communities and in our society in defense of human life. That commitment means that we must be prepared to care for and love those who are terminally ill. Medical professionals can be committed to relieving pain, but they must stand firmly against deliberate actions to end human life. Christian families need to be willing to care for their aging and sick members and to allow them to live out their lives fully for the glory of God. I realize that these are not easy commitments. In fact, they are difficult, expensive, sacrificial commitments, but the alternative is to see our society plunge into a total disregard for human life that is considered unnecessary or too burdensome.

Euthanasia: The "Good" Death That's Not So Good

Physician-assisted suicide is just the first level of a movement toward social approval and practice of euthanasia. The word *euthanasia* means "good death," but it has come to refer to the voluntary and even involuntary termination of human beings who are terminally ill, nonproductive or unwanted.

Some historical perspective might make the issues clearer. In the early decades of the twentieth century, Germany had one of the most sophisticated and progressive medical communities in the world. The ravages of World War I and the financial chaos of the Depression, however, put Germany in a difficult position as a nation. It was heavily in debt to foreign nations; economic activity was stagnant; and the public was ready for national deliverance. On October 15, 1939, six weeks after the invasion of Poland that sparked a second world war, Adolf Hitler dictated a secret memorandum permitting German physicians to kill physically and mentally handicapped patients in German hospitals. Hitler declared 1939 the year of the "Duty to Be Healthy." By the end of the war six years later, 200,000 men, women and children had been killed. Most of the victims were shot, poisoned or starved to death. About a third of those who died were gassed, with methods later used in death camps to kill Jews and other political or racial prisoners.[2]

Two aspects of the Nazi "euthanasia" program are striking.

First, the physicians and the public made little or no protest over the practice. As a whole, German doctors were more concerned with how much butter or meat could be saved for every ward of the state destroyed than with the morality of their actions. The German people had been told for several years that the physically and mentally disabled were people whose lives were unworthy of living. The second aspect of the German program that should slap us awake is that it was a very short step from killing people who were economically burdensome on the state to killing those regarded as enemies of the state. The Jews were demonized as an unnecessary drain on the economy, as criminals, as subhuman beings. Their destruction was justified as an action leading to the greater good of the people. Gypsies, Polish nationalists, homosexuals, Jehovah's Witnesses, dissenting pastors, prisoners of war and even severely wounded German soldiers became "useless mouths to feed" or threatening enemies to eliminate. Many of the bureaucratic and medical professionals who managed the euthanasia program went on to organize Nazi death camps. The techniques for mass murder in the hospitals were quickly adapted for use in the Final Solution.

I don't find it difficult to trace the same pattern in Western nations today. If we accept the practice of physician-assisted suicide, it is just a short step to state-ordered homicide. As our population ages and medical-care costs escalate, more and more of the elderly will be pressured by families or by economic necessity to choose suicide rather than long-term care. As the economic burdens increase, the government and its bureaucracy may find itself pressured by a clamoring public to simply set arbitrary limits on age or medical allowances. When the limits are reached, the person would be allowed to "die with dignity" through lethal injection. The burgeoning prison population and its crippling costs could be severely reduced by wide use of capital punishment. "Three strikes, and you're out" would take on a far more ominous meaning. At that point, the door would be open to the elimination of anyone considered detrimental or burdensome or counterproductive to the greater good of the society. Religious or racial groups would only have to be declared enemies or criminals in order to be exterminated. Probably not a word of protest would be heard from the general population.

Those who are in the racial or religious minority should be the most outspoken in the defense of the value of human life. If you think the scenario I have outlined is impossible in our enlightened society, you haven't learned much from history. If you are considered an economic or social burden, no matter how precious your life might be to you, you will have little chance of surviving.

The Secular Worldview

Physician-assisted suicide and euthanasia rest on a subtle secularist perspective that has permeated our culture—the belief that human life is really no different from animal or plant life, just more highly evolved. If you accept the premise that human life evolved from lower life forms, you can easily conclude that it has no more inherent *value* than the forms from which it came. When a family dog is fatally injured or grows old and sick, we do the compassionate thing and put the animal to sleep. A lethal injection of a drug stops the animal's breathing or heartbeat, and the animal dies. In the secular evolutionary scheme of things, human life is essentially no different from animal life. Therefore, unborn human life that is unwanted or inconvenient can be legally destroyed. Those who are sick or who don't want to live should have the opportunity to choose to die. People who are useless or burdensome to society can be euthanized without any more pangs to the collective conscience than we feel over the thousands of unwanted, unnecessary cats or dogs that are destroyed each day.

If, however, you accept the Bible's declaration that human beings are unique beings who have been created in the image of God, then *human* life takes on far greater significance and value than any other life form. Human life has a sanctity about it that far eclipses animal or plant life. We have a link to God and to eternity that animals do not have. Therefore, if we arbitrarily end human life, born or unborn, capable or disabled, productive or nonproductive, we have touched the image of God in that life—and we incur far greater accountability to God himself. The greatest demonstration of compassion toward a person who is dying of disease or old age is not to end the person's life but to nurture that person and to hold the human life resident in him or her in highest regard.

How Long Do We Prolong Life?

The other side of the issue of euthanasia or terminating life is determining how long we should sustain life that is clearly terminal. Technological advances and strides in medical research have made it possible to sustain the functions of the human body for long periods of time. If an elderly person with congestive heart disease develops pneumonia, should we treat the pneumonia aggressively with antibiotics and a respirator—or should we allow the pneumonia to run its course, knowing that it will bring death to a person who has suffered a long time already?

In my mind there is a distinct difference between *active* euthanasia and *passive* euthanasia. If I inject a lethal drug into the person with congestive heart disease to cause that person to die, I have taken an active course designed to terminate a human life. That approach, I believe, is wrong. If, however,

I do not treat the pneumonia that signals the final stages of life, I have simply allowed the disease or deterioration of age to take its course. Even passive choices are not easy to make. More and more people are writing "living wills" or are communicating clearly to their doctors and families that they do not want "heroic" or unusual measures taken to sustain life in the event of a stroke or heart attack. If there is no reasonable hope of recovery, they simply want to be left in the hands of God.

In my first pastorate, a young woman on her way to work early one morning apparently dozed off and slammed her car into a bridge pillar. The doctors gave her no chance of survival—but she lived. For weeks she was on a respirator in a coma. Finally the family said, "We've decided to unhook the respirator. If the Lord wants her to survive, she will breathe on her own. If the Lord wants her in heaven, she will die." When the respirator was turned off, this young woman began to breathe on her own! Her parents took her home and cared for her for several months, but she never regained consciousness and finally died at home. I do not understand why God allowed Mary to live on those few months, but, for his good reasons, he did.

Some of the issues I've raised in this chapter will tear at the very foundation of our society in the next ten or twenty years. As Christians we cannot speak with the question marks of doubt to a culture seeking direction. We must be prepared to speak with the exclamation points of God's truth, and then be committed to demonstrating sacrificial compassion in our families and in our communities.

Chapter 6

WHAT HAPPENS AFTER I DIE?

*J*im Watkins *writes about hard-hitting issues for young adults.* As preparation for writing a book about death, he surveyed one thousand teens and asked for their questions about death and dying. The most frequently asked question was "Is there really life after death?" Sixth on the list was "Where do you go when you die . . . to a holding tank? . . . to a waiting room?"[1]

The Bible doesn't give us all the answers about the afterlife in one easy-to-read chapter. We have to piece together a few clear declarations and some less obvious clues scattered throughout Scripture. Putting the pieces together rewards us with a deeper understanding of what lies beyond death.

The Shadow of Sheol

In the writings of the Old Testament, the spirits of those who die are said to go to a place called (in Hebrew) Sheol. The word can be found sixty-six times in the Old Testament, and while the biblical writers consistently refer to a person's body as going to the grave, they always refer to the person's spirit as going to Sheol. The person does not cease to exist at death, but his or her soul descends to Sheol.

Unfortunately, the Authorized or King James Version of the Bible translated Sheol as "grave" thirty-one times. Even some modern translations have carried on the tradition of translating Sheol as "grave" in a few instances. This inaccuracy has opened the door for some people to teach that Sheol is *always* a reference to the grave and that the spirits of those who die "sleep" in the grave along with the body. A careful examination of the use of the word, however, demonstrates that Sheol should never be translated as "grave." The Hebrew word for grave was *qeber*. The Old Testament repeatedly refers to the body being buried in a grave (Genesis 23:6; 49:31), but never is a person buried in Sheol.

On the contrary, those in Sheol are conscious. Isaiah said of the wicked king of Babylon,

Sheol from beneath is excited over you to meet you when you come;

It arouses for you the spirits of the dead, all the leaders of the earth;

It raises all the kings of the nations from their thrones.

They will all respond and say to you,

"Even you have been made weak as we,

You have become like us." (Isaiah 14:9-10 NASB)

But not only the wicked entered Sheol. Moses and Aaron were both "gathered to [their] people" when they died (Deuteronomy 32:50), and Jacob despaired at the prospect of grieving for Joseph until he would "go down to Sheol" (Genesis 37:35 NASB).

The writers of Scripture refer to Sheol as "down," "the heart of the earth," or in "the lower parts of the earth" (Genesis 37:35; Ezekiel 32:21; Matthew 12:40; Ephesians 4:9 NASB)—all figures of speech that indicate Sheol is not a part of this earthly realm. It exists in the spiritual realm. Sheol is, nevertheless, a real place where the spirits of human beings went to reside after death.

Jesus Looks Beyond Death

When the Old Testament was translated from Hebrew to Greek, the translators used the word *Hades* to translate the Hebrew word *Sheol.* Jesus used the same word to describe the place inhabited by the spirits of those who had died.

Probably the clearest picture we have of Sheol or Hades comes from Jesus' account of the rich man and Lazarus recorded in the Gospel of Luke.

There was a rich man who was dressed in purple and fine linen and lived in luxury every day. At his gate was laid a beggar named Lazarus, covered with sores and longing to eat what fell from the rich man's table. Even the dogs came and licked his sores.

The time came when the beggar died and the angels carried him to Abraham's side. The rich man also died and was buried. In hell [Hades], where he was in torment, he looked up and saw Abraham far away, with Lazarus by his side. So he called to him, "Father Abraham, have pity on me and send Lazarus to dip the tip of his finger in water and cool my tongue, because I am in agony in this fire."

But Abraham replied, "Son, remember that in your lifetime you received your good things, while Lazarus received bad things, but now he is comforted here and you are in agony. And besides all this, between us and you a great chasm has been fixed, so that those who want to go from here to you cannot, nor can anyone cross over from there to us."

He answered, "Then I beg you, father, send Lazarus to my father's house, for I have five brothers. Let him warn them, so that they will not also come to this place of torment." Abraham replied, "They have Moses and the Prophets; let them listen to them."

"No, father Abraham," he said, "but if someone from the dead goes to them, they will repent."

He said to him, "If they do not listen to Moses and the Prophets, they will not be convinced even if someone rises from the dead." (Luke 16:19-31)

Most Bible teachers refer to this story as the *parable* of the rich man and Lazarus. (The fact that personal names are used for two of the men mentioned—Lazarus and Abraham—makes it unique as a parable.) Unlike fairy tales or fables, parables describe normal events that take place in the real world— farmers sow seeds in fields, prodigal sons leave home, and kings go out to war. This account, then, of events after death can be accepted as an accurate description of what really happened when people died.

In the course of his life, Lazarus, the beggar, had come to believe in the Lord God of Israel. As a result, when he died, the angels carried him to a place of rest and blessing at Abraham's side. The mention of Abraham, the most famous Old Testament saint, makes it clear to Jesus' listeners that Lazarus was in a place where the spirits of righteous people went after death.

In contrast, the rich man had invested himself in the material world alone. When he died, he was probably buried with elaborate ritual and long eulogies. He found himself, however, in Hades—a real "place of torment" (v. 28). Even though the rich man's physical body was in the grave, he could feel the torments of Hades. Jesus said that the man was "in agony in this fire." Jesus also said the man saw Abraham, conversed with him and desired to have Lazarus cool his tongue with a drop of water. Jesus wanted us to understand that this man was fully aware of his surroundings. He even had a clear memory of his previous life on earth. He remembered Lazarus and his five brothers who were still on earth.

Jesus' story of the rich man and Lazarus, the beggar, has led some Bible scholars to portray Sheol/Hades as a place that was divided into two compartments. One side was the dwelling place of the spirits of the righteous; the other side was the place of torment to which the spirits of the unrighteous were sent. Between the two a "great chasm" (v. 26) prevented anyone from moving from one side to the other.

While we can't press the details of the parable too far, several important truths emerge from this story. The most obvious one is that *Jesus believed that death is not the end of human existence.* When we die, we aren't done for! Death is simply the transition from one realm of existence to another. That fact is both comforting and frightening. It's comforting to know for certain that we continue to exist after death, but it's frightening because we have to ask where we will find ourselves one second after death—at rest or in torment.

The second truth Jesus makes clear in this story is that *there are two realms of existence after death.* Human beings go either to a place of rest and comfort or to a place of torment. Jesus never wavered on that fact. The rich man would have been highly regarded on earth. People would have looked at him as a success, and most of us would have been thrilled to have him as a member of our church. But as God meticulously searched this man's heart, he found it empty of faith and obedience toward God. Instead of loving God with all his heart as the Law and the Prophets commanded, this man loved the things he possessed. Instead of loving his neighbor as himself, this man let Lazarus rot on his doorstep. For these reasons, he went to the spiritual realm of torment.

The third truth, a surprising realization to me, was that *the character of the unrepentant doesn't change even in the fire of Hades.* We think that as soon as lost people wake up in hell they will repent and believe in Christ, but that's not true. Men and women who have rejected God's grace in this life will remain unrepentant in eternity. The rich man demonstrated the same attitudes after his death that he had before. The first words out of his mouth were not "God, be merciful to me," but "Send Lazarus to cool my tongue." The rich man thought everything revolved around him before he died, and he wanted it to continue that way after he died. The fact of the matter is that when people have become set in their rebellious attitudes toward God, even death doesn't change them.

Lazarus was not comforted after death simply because he was poor, and the rich man was not tormented simply because he was rich. The rich man was separated from God by his own choice long before he looked up and saw the great chasm separating him from the dwelling place of the righteous. But Lazarus, this poor man who doesn't say one word in the whole story, had a heart that was humble before God. At some time in his difficult life, Lazarus had come in repentance to God and had believed that God's promises were true. In that moment, Lazarus had been born again and declared righteous by faith alone.

A fourth truth to emerge from Jesus' account is that *death is final.* Death seals our eternal condition. All the rich man's requests were denied; all of his pleas came too late. The rich man obviously knew that the place of torment was avoidable. He begged Abraham to send Lazarus back to earth to warn his brothers not to be as foolish as he had been. As the curtain drops on this dramatic scene, a dreadful sense of hopelessness sweeps over the rich man. After death no change is possible. Where you and I spend eternity is not determined after death, but here and now.

When I was a young teenager, I worked in a grocery store in the small town where my family lived. Every Thursday evening I spent several hours with an older man putting prices on the cans and boxes that would fill the store shelves early the next morning. Bill was a notorious sinner, and I did my best to share the gospel with him. His answer to my warnings about future separation from God in hell was always the same: "If I go to hell, all my friends will be there too!" Jesus' story about the rich man certainly shreds that popular myth. The rich man was all alone—and he didn't want his brothers to join him. Far from being like a giant party, hell will be a place of gnawing aloneness.

Did Jesus Go to Hell?

I wasn't raised in a church that used the great creeds of the church as part of the worship service, but I have come to appreciate these compact affirmations of faith as wonderful expressions of what we as Christians believe. There's one phrase in the Apostles' Creed, however, that really bothers me. "I believe," the Creed says, "in Christ Jesus . . . who was crucified under Pontius Pilate and was buried. *He descended into hell.*" That's the part I struggle with. Did Jesus go to hell? Or did he go to the place we've been talking about—Hades? Did he suffer torment like the rich man, or did he spend the days and nights that his body was in the grave in the place of comfort "at Abraham's side"?

The answers to those questions come from an unlikely place—Jesus' promise to a crucified criminal. Jesus was crucified between two thieves, men dying for their own crimes. At first, both men scorned and mocked Jesus (Matthew 27:44; Mark 15:32), but as time passed one man became silent. Finally, in repentance he rebuked the other thief and said to Jesus, "Remember me when you come into your kingdom." Jesus in grace and mercy responded, "Today you will be with me in paradise" (Luke 23:40-43).

The word *paradise* was a Persian word that meant garden or park. It was used by Greek-speaking Jews to refer to the Garden of Eden in Genesis 1—3. The Jewish rabbis used the word *paradise* and the phrase "Abraham's bosom" (or "Abraham's side") interchangeably[2] to refer to the resting place for the spirits of the righteous who had died. So Jesus promised the thief that they would be together in conscious fellowship in paradise that same day. The day of the man's death would be the day of his entrance into the blessing of paradise. But more than that, Jesus said that after his own death *he* would be in paradise too.

Jesus went to paradise for three days before returning in his glorious resurrection. Jesus' presence in paradise prepared the spirits of all those believers who had died since Adam for a glorious transfer—a change of address. Those in paradise left Hades and are today in heaven, in the presence of Christ. When Christ ascended into heaven forty days after his resurrection, he "led captives in his train" (Ephesians 4:8). The hope of every believer in the Old Testament was that God would "redeem my soul from the power of Sheol; for He will receive me" (Psalm 49:15, NASB; see also Hosea 13:14). The "spirits of righteous men made perfect" who are now in the heavenly Jerusalem (Hebrews 12:23) are the believers who died before Jesus' ascension, lived in Hades and now dwell with Christ. When the apostle Paul was taken to the third heaven, the heaven of God, he says that he was "caught up to paradise" (2 Corinthians 12:1-4). When the sacrifice of the cross and the victory of the resurrection were complete, Jesus set the captives free and took his people into the presence of one far greater than Abraham. They are now in the presence of their Redeemer, Jesus Christ.

So Where *Do* We Go When We Die?

The resurrection and ascension of Jesus opened the way into the presence of the Father (Hebrews 4:14; 9:24). Jesus pioneered the way into heaven itself. Every person who has trusted Christ as Savior and Lord enters the presence of Christ immediately on his or her physical death. As Stephen, the first Christian martyr, was being stoned, he "looked up to heaven and saw the glory of God, and Jesus standing at the right hand of God" (Acts 7:55). Stephen's dying prayer was "Lord Jesus, receive my spirit" (Acts 7:59). The apostle Paul wanted "to depart and be with Christ" (Philippians 1:23) because it was far better "to be away from the body and at home with the Lord" (2 Corinthians 5:8).

The resurrection and ascension of Christ made no change in the destiny of unbelievers who die. They still go to Hades, a place of loneliness and torment.

In the opening pages of this book I said that I had seen many people die well and a few die poorly. One of the most disturbing deaths I have witnessed was the death of a man who for years had spurned every mention of Christ or the gospel. He spent the last days of his life in a hospital room, clinging desperately to every tenuous thread of physical life. One day I felt burdened by the Lord to talk to the man once more. When I arrived at the hospital, his room was crowded with family members. His daughter (who was a believer) whispered that the doctor had given her father only hours to live. I leaned over the bed and said, "I've come to ask you again to believe on the Lord Jesus and to be saved by his grace." Before five words were out of my mouth, the man began to shake his head back and forth. He didn't want to hear what I had to say. I moved back to the edge of the room and stood quietly for a few minutes, intending to slip out and be gone. Suddenly the man began gasping for air. His eyes opened wide, and he protested, "No! No! Not yet! Not yet!" His final breath was a long exhalation, and as his spirit departed, his upper body curled downward in a grotesque position.

The family sat in stunned silence. I could barely breathe. I personally believe that at the point of death the man saw his destiny in Hades yawning before him and recoiled in terror.

I realize that this is a troubling account. It makes you really think about your own destiny and that of those you love. You may have a parent or friend or spouse who has died without the Lord. It's painful to think of them being in torment. We may even blame ourselves and say, "If only I had witnessed more or prayed more or tried harder."

A close Christian friend of mine has a deep burden to reach lost people with the gospel. One of his employees had a girlfriend who died of a drug overdose. Through a conversation with the employee, God gave my friend an opportunity to tell him about Christ. At the end of my friend's explanation the grieving man said, "Is my girlfriend in hell right now?"

How is *that* for an awkward question? My friend gave a wise and insightful reply. "The answer has two parts," my friend said. "First, God is the one who judges our hearts, not me. And second, whatever God does is right."

Those who die without Christ have to be left to the Lord. We can't do anything more to change their destiny. But we *can* be motivated to greater faithfulness and courage to share the good news of God's grace with family members and friends who are still alive.

Chapter 7

HELL

The Unquenchable Fire

Y ou might be surprised that Jesus talked more about hell than he did about heaven. Jesus was never afraid of the subject, nor was he ashamed of it. He made it clear to many people on several occasions that he believed in a place of judgment called hell.

Like people today, those in Jesus' day didn't like to be told about hell. Most people don't want to talk, hear or even think about it. The majority of people who have never believed in Christ also refuse to believe in hell as a place of judgment. Our secular society regards hell as an old, worn-out superstition that religious bullies have used to frighten people into submission. Most people just dismiss the possibility that someday they will face eternal fire.

I once asked a Christian friend what he thought about hell before he accepted Christ. "I refused to think about it," he said. "It was just too frightening."

A lot of Christians are also disturbed by the concept of hell. Some believe that God is too loving to send a person to hell. The true God, however, is not only loving but also holy. His love does not contradict his holy hatred of sin and his promised judgment on the sinner.

Other Christians have concluded that human beings are too good to suffer in hell. They contend that God will certainly not allow his own creatures to languish there eternally. They forget that God has declared that we are all desperately wicked before God; we all fall far short of God's righteous standard.

At the other extreme, some Christians emphasize hell. I have heard preachers speak with glee about the everlasting torment of the wicked. What an unbiblical approach! Whenever we talk about hell and about those who are sent there, we need to realize that these are real people who are condemned to eternal separation from God. We should talk about hell with seriousness and even with tears, because hell is what each of us deserves.

I am one of those Christians disturbed by the idea of hell. When I try to comprehend what hell will be like, my mind and heart rebel against every aspect of the doctrine. If the Bible did not make some clear declarations about the reality of hell, I would never be able to believe that hell exists. Jesus taught more about hell than anyone in the Bible. He didn't try to frighten people. He tried to warn them. And he offered faith in himself as the only alternative.

"This Place of Torment"
This chapter explores six closely related facts that summarize the biblical teaching on hell. The first is that hell is a place.

When Jesus told the story of the rich man and Lazarus (re-corded in Luke 16), the rich man said that he did not want his brothers to come to "this *place* of torment" (Luke 16:28).

The Bible describes two distinct places as hell. In Luke 16 Jesus talks about the torment of Hades, the place where the spirits of ungodly people go at death. Their bodies go to the grave and decay, and their spirits go to Hades. The second place described in the Bible as hell is the final lake of fire.

Hades is a temporary place. At the final judgment before God, death and Hades give up the dead in them, and all the dead, small and great, stand before God to be judged (Reve-lation 20:11-15). Nearly all students of biblical prophecy agree that only the lost stand before God at this judgment, sometimes called the Great White Throne Judgment. (Chris-tians and Old Testament believers are judged too but in a different setting.) At the final judgment of Revelation 20 all those who have died in unbelief since the beginning of human history are revived from the dead. They stand before God to be judged "according to what they had done" (Revelation 20:12-13). They are not judged to see if they are saved or lost but to determine their degree of accountability and responsi-bility before God. Perhaps the punishments of hell will vary depending on how much of God's truth an individual under-stood and rejected. One thing is certain—all the works that individuals have done will do nothing more than confirm their lostness before God and their utter inability to earn or merit blessing.

The people who are today in torment in Hades will be resurrected in the future to stand before God. They will not experience the resurrection to *life* but a resurrection to *judg-ment.* Jesus said it this way: "Do not be amazed at this, for a time is coming when all who are in their graves will hear [Christ's] voice and come out—those who have done good will rise to live, and those who have done evil will rise to be condemned" (John 5:28-29). The bodies of those who will be condemned will be raised, but not in glory like the bodies of believers. The resurrection to judgment will result in a reviving of the old body and a reuniting of the body and the spirit. The complete person will then survive forever in hell. When Jesus described the fires of the future hell, he said it was a place "where their worm does not die, and the fire is not quenched" (Mark 9:48). In other words, even though a fire will burn constantly, the revived physical body of the unsaved will not die or be destroyed.

The resurrection to condemnation and the final judgment of God will conclude with an act of ultimate separation. Every unbeliever's knee will bow to Jesus Christ, and everyone will confess that Jesus is indeed Lord (Philippians 2:10-11), and then every person who has rejected God's grace will be ushered into the lake of fire. No description of that place is easy to read. "Death and Hades were thrown into the lake of fire. The lake of fire is the second death. If anyone's name was not found written in the book of life, he was thrown into the lake of fire" (Revelation 20:14-15).

Six times in Matthew's Gospel Jesus described Hades or the final hell as "the fiery furnace," a place of "darkness," or "outside . . . where there will be weeping and gnashing of teeth" (Matthew 8:12; 13:42, 50; 22:13; 24:51; 25:30).

"I Have Five Brothers"
This leads to the second biblical fact: hell is a place of conscious existence. The rich man in Hades was not asleep; he was consciously aware of what was going on. He was able to see, to speak, to feel agony and to remember his life on earth. People in Hades are not annihilated; they do not cease to exist but are fully aware of their condition.

The same will be true of their existence in the final hell. In Revelation 14 the apostle John records the following words of judgment spoken by an angel of God:

If anyone worships the beast, . . . he, too, will drink of the wine of God's fury, which has been poured full strength into the cup of his wrath. He will be *tormented* with burning sulfur in the presence of the holy angels and of the Lamb. And the smoke of their *torment* rises for ever and ever. There is no rest day or night for those who worship the beast. (Revelation 14:9-11)

The Greek word translated "torment" or "tormented" in these verses is used twenty times in the New Testament, five times to refer to eternal punishment, but it always is used to describe *conscious* torment. When Jesus said that those excluded from God's kingdom would go to a place where there would be "weeping" and "gnashing of teeth," he was conveying the idea that people in hell would be fully aware of their condition.

The theologian J. I. Packer suggests that condemned people will focus on four things in hell: "(1) how repulsive and guilty in their Maker's eyes was the way they lived on earth; (2) how right was God's penal exclusion of them from his presence and joy; (3) how completely they have now lost all gladness and pleasure; and (4) how unchangeable is their condition."[1]

"I Am in Agony"

Third, not only is hell a place of conscious existence, but as stated in the Revelation passage above, it is a place of torment. Those who are cast into the final lake of burning sulfur "will be tormented day and night for ever and ever" (Revelation 19:20; 20:10). The Bible teaches that hell is a place of punishment and that the punishment is terrible. It's terrible because it involves exposure to the wrath of a holy and all-powerful God. The writer of Hebrews almost shudders as he writes, "It is a dreadful thing to fall into the hands of the living God" (10:31). Many Christians think of hell as the place of Satan's dominion. Nothing could be further from the truth! Satan hates and fears hell. That will be the place of his final judgment (Revelation 20:10). Satan is not the king of hell; God is.

The Bible pictures hell most often as a place of fire. The rich man in Hades was "in torment," and his own words of testimony are "I am in agony in this fire" (Luke 16:23-24). Hell will mean incredible pain to all sent there.

The term Jesus used most frequently for hell was *Gehenna*. Gehenna is a transliteration of a Hebrew word meaning "valley of Hinnom," which is a ravine on Jerusalem's south side. In the days of Israel's disobedience to God, the valley had been a place of idolatrous worship. Children had been burned there as sacrifices to the Moabite god Molech (2 Chronicles 28:3; 33:6; Jeremiah 32:35). The prophet Jeremiah referred to it as the "Valley of Slaughter" because the people of Jerusalem would be killed there as part of God's judgment on the nation (Jeremiah 7:31-34). Later the valley became the garbage dump for Jerusalem. A fire continually burned in the piles of rubbish. Wild dogs and hyenas roamed the area searching for scraps of food or the bodies of the poor or executed that were thrown there. It became an appropriate picture in the popular Jewish mind for the place of eternal punishment, a place of burning and dread and abandonment.[2]

John in the book of Revelation and Jesus in the Gospels are joined by the apostle Paul in depicting a future judgment on those who reject God's grace. In Romans 2:5 Paul writes that people who hope to be accepted by God on the basis of their good deeds are only "storing up wrath against [themselves] for the day of God's wrath, when his righteous judgment will be revealed." Later in Romans Paul describes those who reject God's gracious salvation as the "objects of his wrath—prepared for destruction" (9:22). One of the clearest statements of the future condemnation of those who reject Christ is found in one of Paul's earliest letters, 2 Thessalonians.

He will punish those who do not know God and do not obey the gospel of our Lord Jesus. They will be punished with everlasting destruction and shut out from the presence of the Lord and from the majesty of his power. (1:8-9)

Christ's judgment on his enemies when he returns will be fierce.

Those Who Do Not Know God

A fourth fact is that hell is the penalty imposed by God on those who don't know God and don't obey the gospel of Jesus. When Paul talks about *knowing God*, he doesn't mean simply believing in some kind of supreme being. He is talking about having a personal, intimate relationship with the one true God, the God who has revealed himself in the Lord Jesus and in the Bible. We enter into that relationship with God by believing the good news that Christ has provided salvation through his death and resurrection. To reject Jesus Christ is to reject the only way that God has provided for salvation.

One Sunday morning several years ago, I ended my message with a simple presentation of the gospel. I emphasized that salvation and eternal life come only one way—through personal faith in the Lord Jesus. It was certainly not unusual for me to make that kind of evangelistic presentation, but a young woman in the congregation that day found it unusual and even offensive. She talked to me after the service through teeth clenched in anger. "That was the most pompous, narrow religious message I have ever heard," she said. "And you are a bigot! How dare you claim that your way to God is the only way!" I had faced this accusation before, so my response was fairly calm. "Your argument is not with me," I said. "Your argument is with Jesus. I only repeated what Jesus himself said." That just angered her more. "Jesus was a compassionate man who loved all people. You have made him into something he is not!" I replied, "Let me read you a couple of things Jesus said, and then you can tell me if I've misrepresented him." I turned to John 14:6 and read Jesus' words: "I am the way and the truth and the life. No one comes to the Father *except through me.*" The young woman was still angry but silent. I added as gently as I could, "I am only as narrow as Jesus was. He said that the only way to God was through him."

Those who claim to love and seek God but who reject Jesus Christ believe in a god of their own imagination, not in the true God. If you reject the message of Christ, no matter how religious or sincere you are, you are still lost, and your destiny is hell.

For Ever and Ever

The fifth scriptural fact is that hell is a place of eternal separation from the conscious presence of God: "They will be punished with everlasting destruction and shut out from the presence of the Lord and from the majesty of his power" (2 Thessalonians 1:9). Jesus confirmed this when he described his own return in Matthew 25. To those who have demonstrated faith in God by the obedient actions of their lives, the King will say, "Come, you who are blessed by my Father; take your inheritance, the kingdom prepared for you" (v. 34). But to those who have demonstrated the absence of faith by the disobedience of their lives, he will say, "Depart from me, you who are cursed, into the *eternal* fire prepared for the devil and his angels" (v. 41). Jesus concluded his remarks by saying, "Then they will go away to *eternal* punishment, but the righteous to *eternal* life" (v. 46). In other words, the punishment of the unrighteous will last as long as the blessing of the righteous—for eternity.

The rich man in Hades was not given any hope that his confinement would be reversed or that the torment of the place would ever subside. Not one verse of Scripture gives any hint that men and women who die apart from Christ are ever given a second chance to believe. Those who are sent to hell will never leave. You can think forward in time until your mind collapses, and that will be just one second of eternity. Hell will never end, and it will never improve.

What keeps my mind secure when I think about the awfulness of hell is the fact that those who spend eternity there have chosen separation from God in this life. They have lived with a focus only on material things and have shown little interest in a relationship with the Lord. When men and women make conscious decisions to reject God's offer of grace, God gives them what they want!

On one occasion in Jesus' earthly ministry, he went with his disciples to an area they had never visited before. A horrible man met them as they arrived. He was naked and scarred, and he shrieked in the agony of demonic oppression. Jesus cleansed the man and restored him to sanity and health, but the people who lived in the area were upset. Jesus had sent the man's demons into a flock of pigs, and the people were upset that the pigs had plunged to their death so that one homeless man could be saved. They were so upset that they asked Jesus to leave, and he did! As far as we can tell from the Gospel records, Jesus never returned to that area again (Mark 5:1-20).

When men and women are confronted with the message of Christ and his power to redeem them from sin's death grip, and they choose to reject Jesus and ask him to leave them alone, he leaves. The everlasting separation of hell will simply be the extension into eternity of that choice made on earth.

Saved from the Coming Wrath

Finally, the sixth wonderful fact is that hell is avoidable.

The Bible declares that *all* of us are lost. We are all sinners by nature and by choice. We deserve the hell the Bible describes. God would be perfectly just and fair if he condemned us all to an eternity separated from him. But in his grace, God has provided a way of escape. God did not provide it because we deserved to be rescued. We didn't deserve it. God provided deliverance from wrath out of his grace alone. God loved us enough to act on our behalf. When we were enemies of God, helpless sinners plunging headlong toward hell, God gave his Son, Jesus Christ, to die on a cross in our place. Jesus took what we deserved. The wrath of God against sin was poured out on Christ.

Jesus died, and he was buried. But in three days he burst from the grave alive. In that one act Jesus broke the power of sin and death and hell forever. He stands today beyond the grave, and he offers salvation freely to all who will believe in him. He gives us life, eternal life—not death, not hell, not what we deserve, but what we *don't* deserve—and we will never perish.

If you have trusted Christ as your Savior and Lord, you are shielded eternally from the wrath of God. You will never experience hell, because Jesus suffered all of it in your place. You have peace with God; you have the Spirit of God within you; and you *have* eternal life right now.

If you are still unconvinced or are tempted to dismiss what God has said, please listen to one more truth. The Christian pastor who wrote the New Testament book of Hebrews was concerned for some people in his congregation who were just like you. They had heard the gospel many times and had even seen the power of God displayed in other people's lives. But they had not personally believed in Christ. They were tempted to reject it all. To paraphrase what the pastor said to them, "Anyone who rejected the Ten Commandments died without mercy simply on the testimony of two or three witnesses. How much more severely do you think a man deserves to be punished who has trampled the Son of God under foot, who has treated as an unholy thing the blood of the cross that sanctified him, and who has insulted the Spirit of grace?" (Hebrews 10:28-29).

If you reject Christ and his offer of salvation, you reject the only sacrifice for sin that's available. Without Christ, you can plan on a certain future in that very real place called hell.

Chapter 8

WHAT ABOUT THOSE
WHO HAVE NEVER HEARD?

*W*henever I speak to people about the eternal destiny of the lost, someone will ask, "What about the person who has never heard about Christ? Will that person be condemned to hell?"

I usually reply that God is the final judge and that he has not assigned any of that responsibility to me! But we *are* responsible to believe what God has told us in his Word. He certainly hasn't answered all our questions, but he does make several truths clear.

The Bible makes it clear, for example, that all humanity is lost. In Adam, we all suffered separation from God. Furthermore, we all have sinned before God, and we all fall desperately short of God's standard of perfection (Romans 3:23). "No one is righteous," declares Paul, "not even one" (Romans 3:10).

The Bible also makes the point that God has revealed enough about his character in the created universe and in the human conscience to make all humanity accountable to him. In the first three chapters of Romans, the apostle Paul brings several types of people before the judgment throne of God to see if they qualify for heaven. The first is the pagan, someone who has never heard the message of Christ. Can that person escape accountability and condemnation? Absolutely not. "For since the creation of the world God's invisible qualities—his eternal power and divine nature—have been clearly seen . . . so that men are without excuse" (Romans 1:20).

Simply by looking at the marvelous universe around them, people who have never heard the gospel can clearly see that God exists and that he is a God of great power. Paul adds in Romans 2 that people who have never *heard* God's law already have it written in their hearts. Having this innate knowledge of right and wrong, people realize that there is a standard of conduct greater than themselves. Their conscience makes them recognize that they are accountable to the same God who displayed his power in creating the universe (Romans 2:15).

If those who have never heard the gospel can see that God exists and that they are accountable to him, won't some of them believe in him and worship him? The overwhelming majority will not. Instead, according to Paul, they "suppress the truth" and turn away from what they know to embrace a lie. They deliberately exchange "the glory of the immortal God for images made to look like mortal man and birds and animals and reptiles" (Romans 1:18-23). When men and women reject the obvious truth about God in order to believe a lie, God lets them go. He "gives them over" to idolatry and immorality and every form of evil—and they love it! "Although they know God's righteous decree that those who do such things deserve [eternal] death, they not only continue to do these very things but also approve of those who practice them" (Romans 1:32).

Will those who have never heard the gospel be condemned eternally? It seems clear to me that they will. Some Christians believe that God in grace will make some provision for those who have never heard. Personally I have difficulty reconciling that belief with the teaching of Romans 1. That position also seems to remove the urgency from proclaiming the gospel to the whole world.

But what if someone *did* respond to the light God has given all humanity? What if someone who had never heard the gospel began to worship the immortal God revealed in the created universe? *If* someone responded, I believe that God would send that person more light.

Early in the book of Acts, a Gentile named Cornelius is called devout and God-fearing, but he had never heard the message of Christ's death and resurrection. So God sent an angel to Cornelius instructing him to send for Peter. Then God gave Peter a vision so Peter would be willing to preach the gospel to a Gentile. Cornelius had responded positively to the limited light he had, and God sent him more light. The moment Cornelius heard the message of salvation in Christ, he believed. Occasionally missionaries tell of a person who hears the gospel for the first time and who responds immediately in faith. Often the new convert will say, "I have found the God I have been searching for. I believe!" Far more often, missionaries who go into areas untouched by the gospel find a wall of unbelief and idolatry that only patience, prayer and the power of the Spirit can overcome.

"But Some *Can't* Believe"

One of the saddest funerals I was ever asked to conduct was

also one of the smallest. A young couple's baby had died a few hours after birth. The parents and I and the funeral director rode to the cemetery together that bright spring morning. The father carried the tiny casket to the grave and then wrapped his arms around his wife. I said a few words, and we cried and slowly turned to leave. At the car the mother asked in a tear-choked voice, "Will I ever see my son again? Will heaven be a place where I will be able to hold him in my arms and watch him grow up?" Her grief was almost unbearable.

I told that mother that I believed she *would* see her child again. I reminded her of the great king David, whose son died in infancy as a judgment of God for David's sin with Bathsheba. When the child became sick, David fasted and wept and prayed before the Lord, thinking, "The LORD may be gracious to me and let the child live" (2 Samuel 12:22). But when his son died, David washed, put on clean clothes and went to the house of the Lord to worship—and then sat down to eat! His servants said, "Why are you acting this way?" David's response has comforted thousands of parents through the centuries. "Can I bring him back again? *I will go to him*, but he will not return to me" (v. 23). David believed that after death he would see his child again.

Does God condemn those who *can't* believe? Infants who die, people who don't have the mental capacity to understand the most basic concepts—are they lost because they have not believed? Given David's words in 2 Samuel and what the Bible tells us about the character of God, I don't think God condemns them. He is a God of grace and justice. His mercy extends particularly to the helpless. It is my conviction that those who cannot believe are given the gift of salvation as an act of God's grace.

This situation is different from those who have never heard the gospel. The apostle Paul says that certain truths about

God are obvious to them, but they reject the light they have. Those who *cannot* believe don't have the capacity to receive God's truth, much less respond to it.

Is It Really That Important?

One warm Sunday afternoon last year I spoke at a Bible conference in our city. For some reason that I still don't fully understand, I talked about the wrath of God and its final expression in the condemnation of eternal hell. A man came up to me after the meeting and said, "Is it really that important that we believe in hell? Can't we focus on the joy of heaven and forget about hell?" My immediate response was "You will have to tear a lot of verses out of your Bible to avoid it." That's certainly one compelling reason to believe in hell; God's Word teaches that it is a real place of judgment.

As I thought about his question, however, I realized that more than the integrity and truthfulness of the Bible was at stake. If we dismiss or question the reality of hell, we seriously undermine the value of the cross of Christ. If there is no future wrath to escape, if there is no eternal condemnation waiting for those who reject the true God, why did Jesus have to die? If we are all simply finding our own way to God and discovering our own religious truth, the cross of Christ is reduced to nothing more than the stirring sacrifice of a man for a good cause. If hell is a real place, however, and the certain destiny of those outside of Christ, the cross becomes the central saving event in human history. God the Son was bearing the abandonment that we deserved. If you want to see the attitude of a holy God toward sin and his treatment of a sinner, look at the cross, because Jesus was made sin for us there.

A refusal to believe what the Bible says about hell has a deep effect on Christians too. First of all, it will drive away our gratitude. The Christian who has lost sight of being delivered from eternal punishment will not rise up in praise and thanksgiving to God for his mercy and grace. Perhaps some of us find praise on our lips so seldom because we have forgotten the misery we deserve and the grace that spared us from it.

Fuzzy thinking about hell will also cause us to lose our sense of urgency about the people we know and love who need the salvation that Christ offers. We may be lulled into thinking that somehow our unsaved friends will find their own way to God. Our willingness to pray for missionaries—and our willingness to give so they can go to the far reaches of the world—will be crippled if we convince ourselves that people are not really lost without Christ.

The biblical truth about hell is not designed to paralyze us; it's designed to motivate us to pray more fervently for the salvation of the lost and to speak more courageously of the love of God displayed supremely in Jesus Christ.

Chapter 9

HEAVEN

The Unspeakable Glory

*S*ome *day you will read in the papers that Dwight Moody is* dead," the great evangelist exclaimed one hot Sunday in August 1899 to a New York City crowd. "Don't you believe a word of it! At that moment I shall be more alive than I am now. . . . I was born of the flesh in 1837; I was born of the Spirit in 1855. That which is born of the flesh may die. That which is born of the Spirit shall live forever."[1]

Four months later, exhausted from years of preaching and labor, Dwight Moody was dying. Early in the morning of December 22, Moody's son Will was startled by his father's voice from the bed across the room: "Earth recedes, heaven opens before me!"

Will hurried to his father's side. "This is no dream, Will. It is beautiful. . . . If this is death, it is sweet. God is calling me and I must go. Don't call me back!"

A few hours later Moody revived to find his wife and family gathered around him. He said to his wife, "I went to the gate of heaven. Why, it is so wonderful, and I saw the children [Irene and Dwight, who had died in childhood]." Within hours the man who had stirred two nations for Christ took a few final breaths and then entered the gate of heaven.

Divine Geography

The Bible always describes heaven as *up*. Paul reminds us that when Jesus came to earth he *descended,* and that when he left earth he *ascended* (Ephesians 4:8-10). The angels told the disciples that Jesus had been taken up from them into heaven (Acts 1:11). When God searches out the faithful, he "looks down from heaven" (Psalm 53:2), and when human beings contemplate God, we look up (Psalm 121:1).

The Bible's portrayal of heaven as above us is, of course, a figure of speech. Heaven cannot be spotted through a telescope or by the cameras of an interplanetary space vehicle. Heaven is in another realm that human observation cannot see or sense. Heaven is a place on God's map, not on the astronomers' star charts.

But that doesn't mean that heaven is imaginary; it is a real place. Jesus told his disciples that he was going to prepare a *place* for them (John 14:2). Heaven is not a dream or a fantasy. In fact, in contrast to earth and the universe around us, which are in the process of passing away, heaven is stable, permanent and eternal (Hebrews 11:8-10).

Our Father's House

"Where is Grandma if she's not here anymore?" Our three-year-old was looking into a casket where his grandmother seemed to be sleeping. "Her body is here for a while," we tried to explain, "but Grandma is in heaven with Jesus." When a believer dies, we say that the person has gone to heaven. The person's spirit is with Christ in a place prepared for them by the Lord Jesus himself. "I am going," Jesus said, "to prepare a place for you" (John 14:2). That "place" Jesus called "my Father's house"—a place of glory and rest and blessing.

Jesus has been preparing his Father's house for two thousand years, and it's already teeming with activity. Three groups inhabit heaven today.

First, heaven is the dwelling place of the holy angels of God. When Jesus was born in Bethlehem, an angel announced his birth to shepherds, and suddenly the sky was filled with "a great company of the *heavenly* host," praising God (Luke 2:13). When the angels left the hillside, Luke says, they went "into heaven" (Luke 2:15). Jesus often spoke of the angels "in heaven" (Matthew 18:10; Mark 12:25; 13:32). When John saw heaven in his vision, millions of angels surrounded God's throne (Revelation 5:11). As the servants of God, angels minister here on earth to those who will inherit salvation (Hebrews 1:14), but they live in heaven.[2]

The second group inhabiting heaven are the spirits of Old Testament believers. When Christ ascended into heaven, he took all the believers who were in paradise or Sheol with him.

The third group in heaven are the spirits of New Testament believers, those who have lived and died since Christ's ascension. You can be confident that after they have died any believers you know will go to join the angels and Old Testament saints in heaven.

The spirits of these dead believers will, of course, also join two others in heaven—Jesus Christ and God the Father.

Forty days after his resurrection, Jesus ascended to heaven. As his disciples stood gaping upward after him, two angels appeared and said, "Men of Galilee, why do you stand here looking into the sky? This same Jesus, who has been taken from you *into heaven*, will come back in the same way you have seen him go *into heaven*" (Acts 1:11). As Stephen was being stoned to death, he looked up to heaven and saw Jesus "standing at the right hand of God" (Acts 7:55-56). Jesus is in heaven today at the place of all authority, and his two activities center on us: he prays for us, and he pleads our case. Romans 8:34 says, "Christ Jesus, who died—more than that, who was raised to life—is at the right hand of God and is also interceding for us." The apostle John writes in 1 John 2:1, "If anybody does sin, we have one who speaks to the Father in our defense—Jesus Christ, the Righteous One." Jesus, as a human being, pioneered the way into the presence of the Father (Hebrews 9:24). Because we have been made clean by his eternal sacrifice of blood we can boldly join Jesus, our intercessor, and come before God (Hebrews 10:19-22).

We realize that heaven does not contain God the Father; he is pure spirit and is greater than his creation. But the Bible pictures heaven as the place where the Father displays his glorious presence. The great lawgiver Moses requests of God, "Look down from heaven, your holy dwelling place, and bless your people Israel" (Deuteronomy 26:15). When Jesus taught his disciples to pray, he addressed God as "our Father *in heaven*" (Matthew 6:9). When human beings are allowed to see into heaven, they perceive God as brilliant light or a burning ember (Ezekiel 1:27; Revelation 4:3). Because God the Father is spirit, he has no body or parts. The Bible uses phrases like "the eyes of God" or "the arm of God" to picture his activity, but in reality God has no arm or eyes. God the Spirit is also pure spirit without a body. Only one member of the Trinity has a body, Jesus Christ. He became fully human at his conception; he was raised to life in a glorified body, and he remains in that body today.

I do not think that we will "see" God the Father in heaven. We will see what John saw—a figure of a person surrounded by brilliant light. The person we will see is Jesus, but we also will see him as John saw him—an awesome, glorious God-man, the exalted Lord of all. We won't run up and shake hands with Jesus when we see him. John was Jesus' closest friend on earth, but when John saw the ascended Lord sixty years after Jesus had gone to heaven, John didn't slap Jesus on the back and say, "It's great to see you again." John fell on his face in adoration and worship (Revelation 1:12-17). In Christ all the fullness of God dwells in bodily form (Colossians 2:9). We will only see Jesus in heaven, but he will be enough.

A New Heaven and a New Earth

As wonderful as heaven is, that present dwelling place of believers is temporary. After the resurrection of believers to life, and after the final judgment on all those who have rejected God's grace, God will accomplish another transformation—not of our bodies but of the universe!

This present universe is under a shroud. Adam's sin affected everything, not just human beings. The ground God had created to produce food abundantly began to require man's toil and sweat before it yielded a harvest (Genesis 3:17-19). The dust, which originally spoke to Adam of the origin of his body and the source of his nourishment, became a symbol of his eventual death—"to dust you will return." The apostle Paul saw the whole creation "groaning as in the pains of childbirth right up to the present time" (Romans 8:22).

Our present earth and the universe around it are in the process of passing away, and someday they will come to an end, not because human beings destroy them but because God does. The apostle Peter tells us exactly what will happen.

> The present heavens and earth by His word are being re-
> served for fire. . . . But the day of the Lord will come like
> a thief, in which the heavens will pass away with a roar and
> the elements will be destroyed with intense heat, and the
> earth and its works will be burned up. . . . The heavens will
> be destroyed by burning, and the elements will melt with
> intense heat! (2 Peter 3:7, 10, 12 NASB)

Peter is describing the total destruction of the earth and the
planetary heavens that surround it. When Christ has reclaimed
the creation that we have corrupted with sin and when he has
conquered every enemy, this present visible universe will evap-
orate with a thunderous roar. The energy held in the atomic
structure of the elements will be released, and the old creation
will melt away.

When the old world is gone, God will step in and create a
new habitation for his people. "But in keeping with [God's]
promise we are looking forward to a new heaven and a new
earth, the home of righteousness" (2 Peter 3:13).

In John's amazing revelation he saw four new things in our
eternal home. He saw a new heaven (Revelation 21:1), a newly
created universe. The word translated "new" in our English
Bible is the Greek word *kainos,* which means newly made. God
will not just patch up this universe. With his awesome power
he will fashion a new universe before our eyes.

John also saw a new earth created, "for the first heaven and
the first earth had passed away, and there was no longer any
sea" (Revelation 21:1). Is this new earth like our present
earth? Probably not. There is no ocean on the new earth, and
later John sees an enormous city resting on it—a city that
would throw our spinning earth out of orbit and into the sun!
God's new earth probably won't rotate, since John says there
is no night there (Revelation 21:25). If the new universe has

a sun and moon, they won't be needed to light the earth since the glorious radiance of God lights it continuously (Revelation 21:23; 22:5). Even though we will dwell in the context of eternity, we will still mark the passage of time, since John is told that the tree of life which flourishes in heaven will bear "twelve crops of fruit, yielding its fruit every *month*" (Revelation 22:2).

Third, John saw that *everything* in the future creation will be new. "He who was seated on the throne said, 'I am making everything new!' " (Revelation 21:5). Heaven will be so unlike what we are familiar with that our present language can't even describe it.

Some things will be missing in the new creation, but they won't be missed. The curse on the old order of living does not apply to this new world (Revelation 22:3). Death, mourning, suffering and pain will be no more, and "[God] will wipe every tear from [our] eyes" (Revelation 21:4). John says that those whose names are written in the Lamb's book of life "will see his face, and his name will be on their foreheads" (Revelation 22:4). No evil, not even the tempter, will lure us away from pure devotion to Christ. Satan's worst nightmare will have come true. He will be confined in the lake of fire to be tormented day and night forever (Revelation 20:10).

The Holy City

The fourth "new" aspect that John saw in his vision of heaven was a magnificent city.

> I saw the Holy City, the new Jerusalem, coming down out of heaven from God, prepared as a bride beautifully dressed for her husband. And I heard a loud voice from the throne saying, "Now the dwelling of God is with men, and he will live with them. They will be his people, and God himself will be with them and be their God." (Revelation 21:2-3)

John describes our future home as a city with walls and gates and streets and rivers, with buildings and people. The new Jerusalem will be a city without flaw, dazzling in its beauty and brilliance, a city whose architect and builder is God (Hebrews 11:10). It is a *holy* city, unspotted by evil and reserved for his holy people. The city is the eternal tabernacle, the dwelling of God and his people forever. John tries to describe the city with reference to the most precious jewels and costliest metals known. The gates are massive single pearls, the foundations are enormous jewels, the streets are pure gold, polished like glass (Revelation 21:18-21).

The angel who escorted John measured the city. Its width and length and height are equal, making a cube that measures fourteen hundred miles on each side. That is roughly the distance from the Mississippi River to the Atlantic Ocean and from the U.S.-Canada border to the Gulf of Mexico and from earth's surface one-twentieth of the way to our moon—the size of a small planet! John doesn't say if the city rests on the new earth or if it's suspended above the new earth or if the city *is* the new earth. It is challenging enough for him simply to try to describe this magnificent eternal home of ours.

John doesn't mention a hospital, since there is no more curse or sickness or pain. He doesn't mention a cemetery, because there is no more death. Another thing John doesn't mention is a church building. Any Christian more committed to a denomination than to Christ might be surprised at the absence of churches, temples and altars, but in this holy city the Lord God Almighty and the Lamb are the temple. Denominational walls will have crumbled, bringing us all together to focus our spiritual activity and worship, not on a service or a building or a doctrine, but wholly on the Father and the Son.

Chapter 10

THE NEVER-ENDING STORY

*W*hen I was a child, I imagined heaven as a place of enormous buildings filled with white-robed people who were total strangers and patrolled by angelic police. Then my grandparents died, and a dear pastor friend died, and my wife's parents died, and Christian friends I had come to love deeply died. I think of heaven now in terms of the people who are there, people I love, people I'm anxious to see again.

We will meet millions of new friends in heaven too. The city has twelve gates, not one—three gates on each side, so people will enter the city from all directions. They will come from all parts of the world, from every level of society, from every direction on the theological compass and from every generation since time began. But we will all be bound together by our faith in and our devotion to the Lord Jesus Christ. Pastor Don Baker in his booklet on heaven said it best:

The Eternal City is for those who have made reservations, for those who have trusted in Jesus Christ, God's Son. Heaven is a prepared place for a prepared people, and preparation is made in the here and now of everyday life.[1]

One question I am asked often about heaven is, Will we know each other there? I think we *will* know each other—and even better than we know each other now. Jesus was recognized by his disciples after his resurrection. When Jesus took Peter, James and John up a mountain and was transfigured before them, the three disciples recognized Moses and Elijah, who came to converse with Jesus. How did they recognize men who had lived hundreds of years earlier? (One teenager in my congregation thinks that maybe Moses and Elijah had "I'm a Visitor" nametags stuck on their robes!) I think the disciples had a taste of the intuitive knowledge we will have in eternity.

I am also persuaded that we will know people as we've known them on earth. I will know my parents as my parents and my children as my children. Even though Jesus made it clear that we will not reproduce in heaven (Matthew 22:30), I think I will know that Karen was my wife on earth. What I'm convinced we *won't* know is who is missing in heaven. Those friends and family members who reject Christ and are condemned will be erased from our memory—along with a memory of our sins and failures and disobedience here on earth. Heaven would not be an experience without tears or pain if we had to live with regret over our past or with remorse for those separated from us. The only person carrying scars into heaven will be Jesus. Even in his resurrection body, the nail scars in his hands and feet and the wound in his side were still visible (John 20:27). Jesus will bear those redemptive scars forever as reminders of what he suffered for our salvation.

Eternity Is a Long Time

If most of us were honest about how we feel about an eternity in heaven, we would have to admit that while heaven sounds like a spectacular place, eternity is a long time. Won't we get bored? The popular image of people in heaven sitting on clouds, strumming harps, doesn't sound like much fun. If you read Revelation 4 and 5, where the redeemed stand before God and worship, you are tempted to think, *That might be fulfilling for the first ten thousand years or so, but is heaven just an endless church service?*

Actually, heaven will be a place of complete fulfillment and challenging activity. The Bible only gives us snapshots of our involvement, but we certainly won't be bored. I find at least five activities that will occupy our minds and hearts and bodies for eternity.

First, we will enjoy *worship without distraction.*[2] Heavenly worship will not be confining or manipulated, but spontaneous and genuine. In Revelation 4 and 5 John sees the throne room of heaven, and arrayed around the Father, the Son and the Spirit are redeemed human beings from every language and tribe and nation. Along with millions of angels and everything in the universe, we shout and sing praise to God—without the distraction of time or other concerns, without the discomfort of physical fatigue and without inhibition. We will lose ourselves in the sheer joy of expressing with our lips the adoration and love we feel for God in our hearts. As you read the book of Revelation, you won't find much preaching in heaven. That bothers those of us who are preachers, but it's a fact. What you *will* find is uninterrupted praise and worship. You won't find quiet, solemn worship clothed in hushed tones and organ music either. Instead you will hear shouts and loud voices and trumpets. We will stand, kneel and fall on our faces—and we won't care what those around us think. All we will care about is that God knows how much we love him.

A second area of involvement in heaven will be *service without exhaustion*. John wrote: "[God's] servants will serve him" (Revelation 22:3). Eight times in the book of Revelation the word *serve* is used to describe our activity in heaven. Maybe that service will be a continuation and expansion of the ministry we have on earth; maybe preachers *will* be called on to preach! Whatever it is, we will be able to serve without frustration or the fear of failure or the exhaustion that so limits our ministries here on earth. The work will be fulfilling, challenging and rich with blessing.

One aspect of that work will be to reign with Christ. Paul told us that we will someday judge the world and even judge angels (1 Corinthians 6:2-3). Jesus pictured faithful servants of God being given charge over particular cities in the kingdom (Luke 19:17-19). Paul promised Timothy that those who endure faithfully will reign with Christ (2 Timothy 2:12). Even in our eternal home "we will reign for ever and ever" (Revelation 22:5). Exactly what form that authority and responsibility will take is not spelled out, but it will be suited perfectly to our abilities and granted according to our faithfulness in the work God gives us to do today.

Fellowship without fear will also occupy us in eternity. We will enjoy the company of thousands of angels, an incredible gathering of Christian believers, millions of Old Testament-era saints, and Jesus himself (Hebrews 12:22-23). We will have time to relax around the table with Abraham, Isaac and Jacob, along with Daniel and Paul and Ruth and Elijah (Matthew 8:11)—and we will have a lot to talk about. We will be able to focus all our attention and energy on others instead of on ourselves.

We won't know everything when we are glorified in heaven, but we will have an infinite capacity to learn. The wonder of *learning without fatigue* will be another of the joys of heaven. Not only will we learn from each other, but we will also be given more and more truth from God. Paul said that in the coming ages God will take us deeper and deeper into a knowledge of "the incomparable riches of his grace" (Ephesians 2:7). Heaven will give us the opportunity to unravel the greatest mysteries of God's abounding grace to us in Christ Jesus.

One of the torments of hell is that there is no rest for its inhabitants (Revelation 14:11). Heaven, however, promises us *rest without boredom* from our difficult labors of earth (Revelation 14:13). Our rest will not be rest from work or weariness; resurrected bodies don't get tired! It will be a rest from want, the empowering rest found in God's presence alone. David wrote with both longing and expectation:

In righteousness I will see [the Lord's] face;
    when I awake, I will be satisfied with seeing [his]
    likeness. (Psalm 17:15)

In heaven we will be perfectly content and satisfied forever.

Chapter 11

RESURRECTION AHEAD

*S*everal *months ago I got a call from a man who told me that* he was selling something everyone needed. He was prepared to give me a great deal on cemetery lots!

I was not in the best mood for a sales pitch, so I said, "Well, you may *think* everybody needs a cemetery lot, but I'm hoping I never need one."

That was followed by a long silence on the other end of the phone line. Finally he said, "Uh, can you tell me why you won't need one?"

I said, "To be honest with you, I'm hoping Christ returns before I die." I have never had a salesperson hang up so quickly.

One of the events we Christians look forward to is the coming of Christ to claim us as his own. Those of us who are alive when Christ returns will not experience death (no cemetery lot needed). Instead we will be instantly clothed with our glorified bodies. I certainly prefer that option to death. But what about all those Christians who have died in the last two thousand years? And what if Christ doesn't return before my death? What happens then?

In Christ's Presence

We've already learned that when a believer in Jesus Christ dies, that person's spirit immediately is in the presence of Christ. To be absent from the body is to find ourselves present with the Lord (2 Corinthians 5:8). Our spirits will remain in conscious fellowship with Christ until a great transformation takes place—the resurrection of our bodies. God created human beings with a physical, material dimension (the body) and with a spiritual, immaterial dimension (the spirit). Our spirits have already been redeemed. We have been regenerated and given new life in Christ. We are not waiting to be made new creatures; we *are* new creatures in Christ (2 Corinthians 5:17). The old things have passed and the new things have come. We don't get eternal life after we die; we *have* eternal life right now (John 3:16; 5:24; 1 John 5:11-12).

Our bodies, however, are still subject to the old order of things. Our outward being is steadily decaying, but our inward being is constantly being renewed (2 Corinthians 4:16). In our inner being we delight in obedience to God, but in our outer being we struggle continually with the flesh, the principle of sin still resident in our bodies (Romans 7:21-23). We find ourselves wanting in our spirit to do what pleases God but so often failing because we yield to the power of the flesh. No wonder even the apostle Paul cried out: "What a wretched man I am! Who will rescue me from this body of death?" (Romans 7:24).

Our full redemption as children of God began when we believed in Christ and were born again; it will continue when our spirits are carried into the presence of Christ at death. But redemption will be complete only when our bodies are resurrected and glorified.

Listen to the declarations of Scripture:

We know that the whole creation has been groaning as in the pains of childbirth right up to the present time. Not only so, but we ourselves, who have the firstfruits of the Spirit, groan inwardly as we wait eagerly for our adoption as sons, the redemption of our bodies. (Romans 8:22-23)

If the Spirit of him who raised Jesus from the dead is living in you, he who raised Christ from the dead will also give life to your mortal bodies through his Spirit, who lives in you. Therefore, brothers, we have an obligation—but it is not to the sinful nature, to live according to it. (Romans 8:11-12)

We know that the one who raised the Lord Jesus from the dead will also raise us with Jesus and present us with you in his presence. (2 Corinthians 4:14)

God's final answer to our cry for deliverance from this body of death will not come when we die and are separated from the body. It will come at the resurrection, when this mortal body we now inhabit will be raised up and transformed. The body of death will give way to a resurrection body. We will spend eternity in glorified human bodies.

The First Resurrection

The person who pioneered the way for us in the resurrection is the same person who walked through the valley of the shadow of death for us—Jesus Christ. Paul says that Jesus was the "firstfruits" of the resurrection (1 Corinthians 15:23). The celebration of first fruits was a powerful image in the minds of the first-century Christians who heard it. Every harvest the Israelites of the Old Testament would take a handful of the first-ripened grain and would wave it before the Lord in expectation of an abundant harvest. Jesus was resurrected in glory as the guarantee of an abundant resurrection of believers later on.

I need to make an important distinction at this point. Many people had been raised from the dead before Jesus' resurrection. During Jesus' earthly ministry he raised three people who were dead—the young daughter of Jairus (Matthew 9:18-26; Mark 5:22-43; Luke 8:41-56), the son of the widow of Nain (Luke 7:11-17) and Jesus' friend Lazarus (John 11:1-44). Elijah and Elisha both were instruments of God to bring a dead child back to life (1 Kings 17:17-24; 2 Kings 4:32-37), and even Elisha's bones brought a dead man to life again (2 Kings 13:20-21). While all those individuals were raised to life, *none* was resurrected. Lazarus and all the others were raised back to the same kind of life they had experienced before their death, and they all died again. But Jesus was raised to a whole new kind of life. His body was transformed, changed, glorified. He would *never* die again! That had never happened before. The apostle Paul almost shouts his affirmation of Jesus' resurrection in Romans 6: "For we know that since Christ was raised from the dead, he cannot die again; death no longer has mastery over him. The death he died, he died to sin once for all; but the life he lives, he lives to God" (Romans 6:9-10).

Jesus as a human being would live forever—and Jesus has chosen to remain a human being eternally. Paul refers to the glorified, risen, ascended Savior as "the *man* Christ Jesus" (1 Timothy 2:5). When the apostle John saw the risen, glorified Son of God in Revelation 1, he saw "someone 'like a son of man' " (Revelation 1:13).

Because Christ lives we will also live (John 14:19). The one who brought Jesus up from the dead in resurrection glory will also give resurrection life to our bodies. Jesus spent three days in paradise in his spirit before his spirit and body were reunited. Our spirits may spend centuries in heaven and our bodies may crumble into dust, but the day will come when the voice of Christ will call those bodies back to life. God will change them, and our spirits will be reunited with our bodies forever.

At the Last Trumpet

God has even told us when this resurrection will take place. Paul hinted at it in 1 Corinthians 15:

Christ has indeed been raised from the dead, the firstfruits of those who have fallen asleep. For since death came through a man, the resurrection of the dead comes also through a man. For as in Adam all die, so in Christ all will be made alive. But each in his own turn: Christ, the firstfruits; then, when he comes, those who belong to him. (1 Corinthians 15:20-23)

The resurrection of "those who belong to [Christ]" will take place "when he comes."

Paul gives us more detailed information when he describes the rapture or the "catching away" of the church in 1 Thessalonians 4. It's a passage that stirs a believer's heart just to read:

Brothers, we do not want you to be ignorant about those who fall asleep, or to grieve like the rest of men, who have no hope. We believe that Jesus died and rose again and so we believe that God will bring with Jesus those who have fallen asleep in him. According to the Lord's own word, we tell you that we who are still alive, who are left till the coming of the Lord, will certainly not precede those who have fallen asleep. For the Lord himself will come down from heaven, with a loud command, with the voice of the archangel and with the trumpet call of God, and the dead in Christ will rise first. After that, we who are still alive and are left will be caught up together with them in the clouds to meet the Lord in the air. And so we will be with the Lord forever. (vv. 13-17)

Apparently some of the Christians were troubled by the fact that a few of the believers had died and Christ had not yet returned. What would happen to these brothers and sisters in Christ? Would they miss the glory of Christ's return? Would they be left behind? Paul puts their minds at ease by explaining exactly what will happen when Christ returns as he promised.

We don't have to grieve about those who have died in Christ. They won't be left out, and they won't be left behind. If the person who died was a believer in Jesus, the funeral and the grave are not the end. The rapture will bring a resurrection, and the resurrection will bring a reuniting of loved ones.

Paul then gives us a great promise—a promise based on the central event in salvation history, the resurrection of Jesus Christ. "We believe that Jesus died and rose again and so we believe that God will bring with Jesus those who have fallen asleep in him" (v. 14). When Jesus returns, God will bring the spirits of those believers who have died back with Jesus.

Those of us still alive when Christ returns will not have the priority in the rapture. We will not get a head start on those Christians who have died. The dead in Christ will rise first (v. 16). The bodies of all those who have died in Christ will be reformed, resurrected to life and glorified—and then reunited with their spirits, which have been in the conscious presence of Christ since the moment of their death. Resurrected believers will be with Christ forever, no longer as spirits but as fully redeemed, glorified, complete human beings.

That's the future confidence of all those who have died in

Christ. But what about those of us who are alive when Christ returns? What happens to us? Paul says that three supernatural events take place.

First, the Lord himself will come down from heaven (v. 16). I don't find any evidence that the return of Christ for his church will be a secret snatching away. The world will know that something is happening; they just won't know what. The Lord will descend with a shout—a military command. At the sound of his voice every believer's body will awaken (John 5:25). Then the archangel will speak, a shout perhaps of triumph and praise. Angels couldn't keep silent at Jesus' birth when redemption's plan began; they may explode in praise again when redemption is completed. Finally will come a trumpet blast, a call to assembly.

We have already discussed the second supernatural act in this divine drama—the dead in Christ will be resurrected in glory (1 Thessalonians 4:17). The third supernatural event will be the transformation of believers who are still alive on earth when Christ returns. We will simply be changed and then caught up in the clouds to meet the Lord. The word translated "caught up" in 1 Thessalonians 4:17 means a sudden, forcible seizure. So we will be grabbed out of the world by an irresistible act of God. We will meet the Lord in the air as fully redeemed, glorified children of God, prepared to spend eternity in Christ's presence. We will be with those who have died in Christ, and we will remain with the Lord forever.

The entire drama of the rapture will take place in a moment of time: "Listen, I tell you a mystery: We will not all sleep, but we will all be changed—in a flash, in the twinkling of an eye, at the last trumpet. For the trumpet will sound, the dead will be raised imperishable, and we will be changed" (1 Corinthians 15:51-52). In the time it takes for the sound of the trumpet to fade away, it will all be over.

If you are like me, you can't read these great promises of Scripture without asking, "When will all this happen?" The answer is that Paul didn't know. God had not told him! The *fact* of Christ's coming is certain; the *time* of Christ's coming is a mystery known only by God. Paul believed that Christ could come during his lifetime. He told the Thessalonians that he hoped to be among those still alive when Christ returned. He said, "*We* who are still alive and are left will be caught up" (1 Thessalonians 4:17). Don't be deceived by those who claim to have figured out when Christ will return—and who want to sell you a book or a videotape that lets you in on the secret! God could have revealed the date of Jesus' coming as precisely as he revealed the order of events at his coming, but God has chosen not to do that. We are to live our lives as if Jesus could return for his people at any moment.

You may believe that after the rapture the world will be plunged into a period of chaos that will end only when Christ returns visibly to earth to set up a kingdom of righteousness. You may believe that the rapture will be part of the final end of human history. The purpose of this book is not to debate the order of end-times events. What we should all be concerned with, regardless of our views on the events of the last days, is this admonition from the apostle John: "Dear children, continue in him, so that when he appears we may be confident and unashamed before him at his coming" (1 John 2:28). John adds later, "Everyone who has this hope [of Christ's return] in him purifies himself, just as he is pure" (1 John 3:3).

When I was a teenager, my parents would say to me before I left home for an evening with my friends, "Go places where you could invite Christ to go, and do things you would not be ashamed of doing if Christ were to return." I thought it was corny back then, but back then I wasn't very wise. Today it sounds like very wise counsel.

Chapter 12

OUR FINAL
REWARD

*O*ur *five-year-old son came as God's "surprise package" when* Karen and I were forty. He's a handful for his dad to keep up with sometimes. Last night we had a wrestling bout on the living-room floor. After twenty minutes of mock battle interspersed with a lot of tickling, Kyle showed no signs of tiring. I lay back on the floor and said, "Okay, Kyle, that's enough. You win. Daddy is worn out."

Kyle put his hands on his hips, leaned over my face and said, "Is this what it's like to be old?"

The truth is that our physical bodies wear out. We may be strong and full of energy when we are young, but the years soon begin to take their toll. There is some good news, however. Someday this body will undergo a dramatic change. The resurrection and glorification of the believer's body will equip us to live eternally.

A New Body

Whenever I speak on our future resurrection as believers, I can count on one question from the audience: "What will our resurrection bodies be like?" The Bible doesn't answer every question we have about our future bodies, but it does give us enough information to make us look forward with wonderful anticipation to our transformation.

We can learn about our resurrection bodies first by examining what the Scriptures tell us about Jesus' resurrection body. The apostle John writes this: "Dear friends, now we are children of God, and what we will be has not yet been made known. But we know that when he appears, we shall be like him, for we shall see him as he is" (1 John 3:2). When Jesus appears we will be resurrected or transformed to be *like him*. Paul adds in Philippians 3:21 that Christ "will transform our lowly bodies so that they will be like his glorious body." We are being transformed right now in our *spirits* into the image of Christ (2 Corinthians 3:18); someday our *bodies* will be made like his too.

The second source of information about our resurrection bodies is 1 Corinthians 15—a detailed explanation of the transformation that will take place in the future. After defending the absolute necessity of the resurrection of Jesus and the guaranteed certainty of our resurrection, Paul launches into a description of the continuity between our present bodies and our future bodies—*and* the amazing contrasts between the two bodies.

The resurrection body will have a connection to the body that dies, like the connection between a seed that is planted and the new plant that emerges: "When you sow, you do not plant the body that will be, but just a seed, perhaps of wheat or of something else. But God gives it a body as he has determined, and to each kind of seed he gives its own body" (1 Corinthians 15:37-38).

If you plant a seed in the ground, the seed dies, but a new life, a new body, emerges. It is different from the seed in some ways, but in some ways it is the same. Jesus, when he rose from the dead, was recognized by his disciples as Jesus (except when he deliberately hid his identity from the two followers walking to Emmaus). He looked essentially like he had looked before. But Jesus' body also had some different qualities—he could pass into a room without opening a door (John 20:19). Yet he could eat food (Luke 24:42-43). He could be touched; his body had substance (Luke 24:39; 1 John 1:1). There was continuity between the first body and the resurrection body.

The same will be true in our resurrection. I think we will look essentially the same, but there will also be some changes. We can't begin to comprehend those changes any more than by looking at a kernel of corn we can envision what a fully grown cornstalk will look like. I am convinced that the effects of sin and the curse will be removed—no eyeglasses or wheel-chairs or respirators will be needed. I *hope* that I'll have more hair and a smaller waist measurement! But we will be able to function much like Jesus functioned as a resurrected man. We will eat at the great marriage supper with Abraham, Isaac and Jacob (Matthew 8:11), and we will drink wine with Jesus in commemoration of his death for our redemption (Matthew 26:29). Jesus told John that there would be no more death or crying or pain, because the old order of things will pass away (Revelation 21:4).

Paul also draws some contrasts between our present bodies and our future bodies. In 1 Corinthians 15 I find five of them. First, our present bodies are perishable, while our resurrection bodies will be imperishable. Our new bodies will not decay, deteriorate or degenerate; we won't grow old. Second, our present body is marked by dishonor; we bear the scars of sin. Our new body will be a body of glory and radiance. The third contrast is the one I like best. Our present body is characterized by weakness; we get tired and sick. Our resurrected body will be characterized by power—dynamic, self-sustaining energy. Fourth, Paul writes that the current body "is sown a natural body, it is raised a spiritual body" (v. 44). That doesn't mean we will float around like a spirit or a ghost. It means that our present bodies are dominated by the flesh, while our resurrected bodies will be controlled by our redeemed spirits. We won't struggle with temptation or lust or greed. Paul's final contrast is drawn from verses 45-49.

> The first man Adam became a living being; the last Adam, a life-giving spirit. . . . The first man was of the dust of the earth, the second man from heaven. As was the earthly man, so are those who are of the earth; and as is the man from heaven, so also are those who are of heaven. And just as we have borne the likeness of the earthly man, so shall we bear the likeness of the man from heaven.

Our present bodies bear the image of Adam, a noble being created in the image of God but fallen in sin. Our resurrection bodies will bear the image of Jesus Christ, the Lord of glory and the faithful Son of the Father.

Giving an Account

God's promise to us of a future resurrection is designed to bring us comfort in life's storms and hope at death's door. One further aspect of our future resurrection also produces motivation toward holy, faithful living. The New Testament tells us that we as believers will give an account of our lives before Jesus himself. Jesus' evaluation of us will not be to see if we are saved or lost. That issue was settled when we believed on the Lord Jesus and received eternal life by his grace alone. There is no condemnation now or in the future to those who are in Christ Jesus (Romans 8:1). The evaluation we will face will be an evaluation of what we did in life with the gifts and opportunities God gave us. The results of that evaluation will bring us either reward or the loss of reward.

We need to look first at three clear New Testament descriptions of the future judgment seat of Christ.

For we must all appear before the judgment seat of Christ, that each one may receive what is due him for the things done while in the body, whether good or bad. (2 Corinthians 5:10)

You, then, why do you judge your brother? Or why do you look down on your brother? For we will all stand before God's judgment seat. . . . So then, each of us will give an account of himself to God. (Romans 14:10, 12)

By the grace God has given me, I laid a foundation as an expert builder, and someone else is building on it. But each one should be careful how he builds. For no one can lay any foundation other than the one already laid, which is Jesus Christ. If any man builds on this foundation using gold, silver, costly stones, wood, hay or straw, his work will be shown for what it is, because the Day will bring it to light. It will be revealed with fire, and the fire will test the quality of each man's work. If what he has built survives, he will receive his reward. If it is burned up, he will suffer loss; he himself will be saved, but only as one escaping through the flames. (1 Corinthians 3:10-15)

In the passage from 1 Corinthians 3, Paul uses the picture of a building to illustrate every believer's responsibility before God. God is building a great building. The foundation has already been laid in the saving work of Jesus Christ. The blueprint has already been approved; we build according to the grace that God has given us—and each one of us is building. This is not a passage directed only at pastors or Christian leaders. Whether you know it or not, whether you like it or not, you *are* building. That's why Paul warns: "Each one should be careful *how* he builds" (1 Corinthians 3:10).

You can use eternal things to build with, or you can use worthless things. Gold, silver and costly stones refer to the fruit of the Spirit in our lives; they refer to Christ-honoring motives and godly obedience and transparent integrity. Wood, hay and straw are perishable things—carnal attitudes, sinful motives, pride-filled actions, selfish ambition. If you are seeking to serve God with commitment and faithfulness and obedience, you are building with the right stuff; if you are coasting along with no desire for spiritual growth or sacrificial ministry to other believers, you are building on God's house using the wrong stuff.

It's vital that you and I make an honest, eyes-open evaluation of our lives, because someday we will each stand before Christ and give an account to him of *how* we have built. My part on the building will be examined by the Lord Jesus and will be tested by the fire of his heart-searching gaze (see Revelation 1:14). That fire will expose and destroy all the things I have done in selfish ambition and with wrong motives. Some of those things may look outwardly to be very noble and even sacrificial, but Jesus will expose the secret intentions behind them. On the other hand, the fire will expose other actions as true acts of humility and Christlikeness, even though at first they appeared to be insignificant. You and I will be rewarded on the basis of what remains. The gold, silver and costly stones of obedience and faithfulness and sacrifice will represent our rewards, our victor's crowns.

The idea of the judgment seat comes straight out of the

athletic games of Paul's day. After the races and games concluded, a dignitary or even the emperor himself took his seat
on an elevated throne in the arena. One by one the winning
athletes came up to the throne to receive a reward—usually a
wreath of leaves, a victor's crown. Some Christians are both-
ered by the idea of such rewards or crowns for faithful believers! Paul certainly wasn't ashamed to strive for crowns of
reward. He wrote this at the end of his life to his friend
Timothy: "I have fought the good fight, I have finished the
race, I have kept the faith. Now there is in store for me the
crown of righteousness, which the Lord, the righteous Judge,
will award to me on that day" (2 Timothy 4:7-8).

According to 1 Corinthians 3:14-15, some of us will receive
rewards and some of us will experience the loss of our rewards. Christ will show us what *could* have been our reward
if we had served him faithfully, but all we will have to offer
him will be ashes, the burned-up remains of laziness or selfish
motives. What a tragedy to stand with empty hands before
Christ, who gave up his own life for us. We will be saved—
but unrewarded. I've wondered sometimes what our excuses
will sound like as we look at his nail-pierced hands.

A Worthy Ambition

Shortly after I became the pastor of a church in western Mich-
igan, a woman asked me what my goals were for the ministry
there. I perceived that the question was asked seriously, so I
answered seriously. I had seen incredible potential for that
congregation in a number of areas of ministry, and I began to
lay out my dreams and desires of what I believed God would
do. At the end of my response to her question, she said, "I
think you are an ambitious man! I don't like that in a pastor."
My reply was "I hope that my ambitions are centered only in
doing what will bring glory to God, not glory to myself."

I've thought a lot about that woman's attitude toward ambition since then, and I have concluded that she was totally wrong! We as believers *should* be ambitious, energetically and boundlessly ambitious—to do one thing, to please Christ.

Paul was an ambitious man. He had one overriding, all-encompassing passion in life, and everything he did was measured against it. His own words explain it best: "So we make it our goal to please [Christ]" (2 Corinthians 5:9). The question Paul asked himself constantly was "Am I pleasing Christ?"

That's a good question to ask yourself! Is my conduct where I work pleasing to Christ? Will what I read or watch on television tonight please Christ? Do my spending habits honor Christ? Am I willing to give an account to Christ of my behavior on a date or on a business trip? We had better be willing to give an account to Christ, because we *will* give an account: "For we must all appear before the judgment seat of Christ" (2 Corinthians 5:10). What will matter is not whether we have pleased ourselves but how well we have pleased Jesus Christ.

The apostle Paul did not serve Christ out of fear or force. He just said, "If someone as wonderful as Jesus could do all that he did for someone as unworthy as I am, how can I take love like that for granted and live only for myself? What else can I do but kneel before the One who died for me and give him all that I am and all that I have and all that I ever hope to become?" Paul was willing to serve Christ to the point of death.

Unfortunately, we've lost sight of the immensity of Christ's love for us. We hear the message of God's grace, and, instead of breaking us, it bores us. We've reduced the love of God and the cross of Christ to neatly tied theological packages, but we are years removed from any fresh experience of God's power in our lives. We are cold and predictable in our ministries and in our praying and in our pleading with lost people because we've forgotten the grace that was required to save us.

The judgment seat of Christ is not an encounter we should fear. We will face the person who loves us most, and his perfect love casts out our fear. But the fact that we will give an account of our lives to Christ should make us realize how serious the Lord is about how we live our lives as his children. I don't know what might be hindering you from cultivating a walk of godliness, but whatever it is, I would urge you to lay it aside and, in the power of the Holy Spirit, determine to live in obedience to Christ. I don't know about you, but I want to face Christ without shame.

Chapter 13

COMFORT FOR THOSE LEFT BEHIND

*A*s comforting as God's promises are to those who are dying, those of us left behind often aren't very comforted. Our parent or spouse or child or friend still dies! Our separation from that vital person in our lives can be devastating.

Many times I have listened to people who come to me a few weeks or months after a funeral and say, "We aren't handling this very well. We believe what God says about the person who has died, but we are collapsing!" Their feelings toward God span a wide range from anger ("why would God do this?") to guilt ("is it my fault?") to despair. Most Christians caught in the backwash of sorrow find it hard to pray.

How can those of us who are left behind deal with the loss and grief of death? Are there any promises from God for *us*?

I've always found it fascinating that the key passages in Scripture about death and what lies beyond death are written not so much to prepare the dying as to comfort the living. After Paul's long discussion about the resurrection and glorified bodies in 1 Corinthians 15, he concludes by challenging living Christians to courageous dedication. "Therefore, my dear brothers, stand firm. Let nothing move you. Always give yourselves fully to the work of the Lord, because you know that your labor in the Lord is not in vain" (v. 58).

Paul's instruction about the rapture of the church and the coming of Christ was not given simply to satisfy the curiosity of Christians about the future; it was designed to encourage and strengthen believers who were struggling with the deaths of loved ones (1 Thessalonians 4:18). Knowing the truth about what has happened to those who have died in the Lord brings comfort to those left behind and helps us press on with our lives rather than get bogged down in despair and grief.

Good Grief

One of the best things you can do when a family member or friend dies is to give yourself and others the freedom to grieve over the separation that death brings. I get a little annoyed at Christians who say to other Christians who are dealing with the death of someone they loved, "You shouldn't be crying! You should be rejoicing. That person is in heaven." These are the same people who bombastically say, "The funeral shouldn't be sad or somber; it should be a victory celebration!" I understand the desire of people like that to focus attention on the promises of God and the glories of heaven, but their approach makes me cringe. Yes, the believer who has died *is* in heaven—and we *will* see him or her again someday—but we are still human. We still feel sorrow and loss and separation. Paul made it clear in 1 Thessalonians 4:13 that we don't grieve as those who have no hope, but we *do* grieve! When Stephen, the first Christian martyr, died, "godly men buried [him] and mourned deeply for him" (Acts 8:2). Sorrow in the face of death is not a lack of faith but part of the healing process. I've discovered in dozens of funeral homes that words alone are not what comforts people overwhelmed with grief; they are comforted when we follow the biblical command to "mourn with those who mourn" (Romans 12:15). A funeral without sorrow is the funeral of a person who lived a life totally alone.

Joe Bayly had three sons who died. The first died when only eighteen days old after an emergency surgery. Another died of leukemia at age five. The third died when he was eighteen years old after a sledding accident. Joe wrote an excellent little book before his own death in 1986 entitled *The Last Thing We Talk About.* In it he describes how we can comfort the mourner.

When Job's friends came to see him after his children died and he had suffered in so many other ways, they missed the opportunity to go down in history as uniquely sensitive and understanding. There they sat on the ground with him for seven days and nights, and they didn't say a word, because they saw how utterly grief-stricken he was. But then they began to talk and spoiled it all. . . .

Don't try to "prove" anything to a survivor. An arm about the shoulder, a firm grip of the hand, a kiss: these are the proofs grief needs, not logical reasoning.

I was sitting, torn by grief. Someone came and talked to me of God's dealings, of why it happened, of hope beyond the grave. He talked constantly, he said things I knew were true. I was unmoved, except to wish he'd go away. He finally did.

Another came and sat beside me. He didn't talk. He

didn't ask leading questions. He just sat beside me for an hour or more, listened when I said something, answered briefly, prayed simply, left. I was moved. I was comforted. I hated to see him go.[1]

Grief and sorrow are never fully overcome until they are expressed. We need to give other people (and ourselves) an atmosphere of freedom in which to express those feelings. Some of us have the attitude that if someone in the depths of pain says something that sounds unspiritual, we have to jump in and get our Bible and set the person straight. We use God's promises to club people, not comfort them. As Christian brothers and sisters we need to pay close attention to the words we use with those who are grieving. I don't know of any other situation that requires sensitivity to the Holy Spirit like the encounters we have in funeral homes. I do not enter a funeral home or hospital room or home bedside where death has occurred without asking God for the wisdom to say the right words and then to be silent.

In Memory of . . .

Another avenue for dealing with the sorrow death brings is to focus on planning a funeral or memorial service that exalts the Lord Jesus and that speaks to the living about the life Jesus offers. As a pastor, I regularly encourage Christians to think about their funeral service and to write down some of the elements they want included in that service. Several months ago, Leah Stacey died after two years of illness. Her daughter gave me Leah's Bible to use in preparing for the service. Tucked in its well-worn pages were lists of hymns and Scripture passages—and a handwritten note that Leah wanted read at her funeral. If you think that was simply the morbid obsession of an old woman, you are wrong. This dear child of God wanted to live out the New Testament principle that whether in life or in death she would glorify Christ Jesus (Philippians 1:20).

In my files I have written instructions from several people about their funeral services. I've even talked with my parents about their desires, as difficult as that was to do. I helped my mother paint her living room one sunny spring day, and we talked about all kinds of issues. Would she remarry if Dad died? Would she want Dad to remarry if she died first? What would she want said and done at her funeral? It seemed easier to talk about these things when we didn't have to look face-to-face—and when my mother couldn't see all the times my eyes filled with tears. My dad has said several times that he wants to be buried in pajamas and a housecoat, not a suit. "My body is asleep—and that's the way I sleep!" I always thought it was a strange request until my father's father died a few years ago and in the casket his body was clothed in pajamas and a robe. He looked at rest dressed like that, ready to be clothed with the brilliant garments of the redeemed.

Christian families need to make it clear to the pastor who speaks at the funeral that they want the focus of the service to be not so much on the person who has died as on that person's Lord and Savior. Funerals are wonderful opportunities for the presentation of the gospel. More than once, on the day family and friends have gathered to commemorate a person's death, someone listening to the message has found life in Jesus Christ.

If your parents or spouse or children are still alive, one of the best things you can do is to say to them what you want them to hear from you if you were to die tomorrow. We somehow think that there will be plenty of time and abundant opportunities to express our love and appreciation to those dearest to us, but that may not be the case. When I lived away from my parents, I would write them each a birthday letter every year. I would try in those letters to express the feelings in my heart for them as parents and as friends. Now that I live close to them, I try to express my love in actions as well as in words. If you have a broken or strained relationship with your parents or a child or a sibling, be the one to take the initiative to attempt a reconciliation. I realize it may not be easy, but you can't speak words of love or apology or appreciation to a fresh grave. All that come out are words of regret.

Dealing with the Body

Some of the most controversial decisions families must make center around the body of the person who has died. Should the casket be open or closed? Is cremation an option, or is burial preferred?

Some Christians have taken a low view of the body. I actually heard one Christian say to his family, "When I die, just put my body in a dumpster and save the cost of a funeral!" But this body of ours is part of our created being. Throughout the Bible, God's people have treated the bodies of those who have died with respect and honor. Abraham buried Sarah in a cave that later became his burial place (Genesis 23:1-20; 25:8-10). Joseph asked that his bones be buried in the land of God's promise, not in Egypt (Genesis 50:25-26; Exodus 13:19; Joshua 24:32). Jesus' followers put their own lives at risk by asking for Jesus' body and placing it carefully in a rock tomb (John 19:38-42). The body is an empty tent without the human spirit living in it, but it was a temple of the Holy Spirit during our earthly life (1 Corinthians 6:19-20) and the only way those who knew us and loved us could recognize us. I certainly don't advocate pagan veneration of the body, but I think we as Christians should treat it respectfully.

The consistent practice of Christians for two thousand years has been to bury the bodies of those who have died, either in a tomb or in the ground. Early Christian cemeteries were called "dormitories" or sleeping areas since the bodies were asleep, waiting for the daybreak of the resurrection. Just as Jesus' body was buried, our bodies are planted in burial in anticipation of the day when those bodies will be raised in glory.

Occasionally a Christian family asks me about cremation as a means of dealing with the body after death. The Bible does refer to the burning of the body after death, but never in a very positive light. Cremation was part of the judgment placed on serious offenders of the law in the Old Testament. The sins of incest and of prostitution by a priest's daughter were punished by death in the fire and the burning of the body (Leviticus 20:14; 21:9). Achan and his family, who violated God's ban on removing wealth from the city of Jericho, were stoned, and then their bodies were burned (Joshua 7:15, 25). When God judged Korah and his followers for their rebellion against Moses and Aaron, "fire came out from the LORD and consumed the 250 men who were offering the incense" (Numbers 16:35). The bodies of King Saul and his sons were burned by the Israelites in Jabesh Gilead, probably to prevent further abuse and mutilation of the bodies by the Philistines. Saul's bones were later buried under a tamarisk tree (1 Samuel 31:12-13).

Cremation was preferred over burial by the Romans during the New Testament era and beyond. Dignitaries were cremated at various places along the Appian Way, and shrines, many still visible today, were set up in their memory. The early Christians shunned the practice of cremation, preferring to bury or entomb the bodies of believers in the great network of catacombs under the city of Rome. If Christians were burned at the stake, other believers would gather their ashes or bones and bury them.

While the preference of Scripture and tradition is to bury the body, there is no direct prohibition of cremation in the Bible. Some secularists and haters of God have had their bodies cremated in an attempt to avoid any future resurrection or judgment of God, but God's power is certainly not limited by the puny efforts of people to escape his promise of judgment. Many believers have been buried at sea or killed in battle, and their bodily remains have been dispersed into the earth or water. That will not hinder God from reclaiming and resurrecting their bodies. The present body is just a seed of the future glorious body. Cremation simply speeds the process of deterioration to the dust from which the body originally came.

I can recall only one person in my ministry who wanted to be cremated. Betty was a beautiful woman whose body was ravaged by cancer. At her funeral the casket was closed, and a picture of her "B.C." (before cancer) self was displayed on top. She had instructed her family to have her body cremated after the service and to bury her ashes in the cemetery. She talked this over with me months before she died. "My body bears the marks of sin's destructive power," she said. "I know it all will be removed in the resurrection, but this is my way of putting my 'Amen' on Jesus' victory over the worst that sin can do to us." Betty had made a decision not based on defiance of God, but as a declaration of faith in God. I was not going to stand in her way.

The God of All Comfort

Don and Clara Munro, like most parents, assumed that their two sons would someday bury them. Instead, their oldest son died in his early forties. Several months after young Don's death, we sat in my office, and I listened to words I had heard many times from grieving people but that came with fresh tears and piercing sorrow. Here were two believers who knew the promises of God about death and were willing to believe God's Word and yet were finding it difficult to carry on with life. "We find ourselves crying at the oddest times. One little thing—a picture, a memory, something on television, a holiday—will bring a whole new wave of sorrow. But what's worst of all is that we can't seem to pray. We get a few words out and can't go on."

I tried to assure these dear friends that they were feeling what many Christians experience in the aftermath of death. It was not a lack of faith or a matter of toughing it out; they were working through the depths of grief that often don't surface until the shock of death subsides and the loneliness of separation sets in. My words sounded hollow that day. I wished I could have helped them more.

A few days later Clara told me that a Christian friend had said something that had really encouraged her, especially about her inability to pray. "Clara," she said, "you have prayed many times for people who have had needs or who have faced sorrow. Now people are praying for you. This is one of those times when the prayers of others carry you."

When a person dies, we all gather around the family for support and encouragement, and we *should* do that. But the time when those people really need us may be weeks or even months later, when the grinding loneliness and even despair set in. Ours is "the God of all comfort, who comforts us in all our troubles" (2 Corinthians 1:3). When we let him, he will use human hands and human hugs to convey that comfort to hurting people.

Heaven on Earth

Something we sometimes forget when we think about heaven is that we as believers have the potential to live a heavenly life right now. In Ephesians 2:6 Paul says that we are already seated in the heavenly realms in Christ Jesus. We are heirs of all of God's riches, and in the Holy Spirit who lives within us we have the down payment on our inheritance (Ephesians 1:13-14). We have the blessings of fellowship with God right now. All the activities that will occupy us in eternity can fill our lives every day. Eternal life doesn't start when we die; it started the moment we believed in Christ. We possess a whole new kind of life in him!

A lot of Christians look at heaven and think it will be eternally boring because their Christian lives here are boring. But if your walk with Christ is uneventful and unexciting and unfulfilling, it's because you haven't laid claim to the resources that God has already promised and provided. We have the Word of God to lead us and encourage us—but we don't invest much time in it. We have the power of God's Spirit resident within us—but we aren't cultivating any relationship with the Spirit. We have the fellowship of believers to stimulate us to consistent and faithful living—but we don't even get involved in other people's lives.

Every day provides fresh opportunities to invest in eternal things. What amazes me is how God can use our smallest efforts at times to produce abundant results. My father pastored a church near Detroit in the late 1950s. Several decades later my parents were invited back to that church for an anniversary celebration. A man came up to my father and said, "You don't know me, but I know you. When you were the pastor here, you made a hospital visit one day to a man from your church. I was in the bed next to that man. As you read Scripture and had prayer with him, the Lord convicted my heart. That was the thing that brought me to Christ." The man was actively involved in the ministry of that church.

My desire and prayer is that this book will stir us to godly and holy living today. That's what God wants his truth to accomplish in each of us. He hasn't told us about heaven's glories so we will dress in white robes and sit on a mountaintop waiting for Jesus to come. He has told us what lies ahead so we will live courageous lives here and now. I can't say it better than the apostle Peter:

Since everything will be destroyed in this way, what kind of people ought you to be? You ought to live holy and godly lives as you look forward to the day of God and speed its coming. . . . So then, dear friends, since you are looking forward to this, make every effort to be found spotless, blameless and at peace with him. (2 Peter 3:11-12, 14)

Notes

Chapter 1: I'm Afraid of Dying!
[1]Ken Gire, *Instructive Moments with the Savior* (Grand Rapids, Mich.: Zondervan, 1992), p. 75.

Chapter 2: Why Do We Have to Die?
[1]Sherwin Nuland, *How We Die: Reflections on Life's Final Chapter* (New York: Alfred A. Knopf, 1994).

Chapter 3: The Lie at the End of the Tunnel
[1]For a detailed evaluation of *Embraced by the Light* from a biblical perspective, see the InterVarsity Press booklet I wrote, *Deceived by the Light* (Downers Grove, Ill.: InterVarsity Press, 1995).
[2]Betty Eadie, *Embraced by the Light* (Placerville, Calif.: Gold Leaf, 1992), p. 46.
[3]For an extensive discussion of the scientific and biblical issues surrounding near-death experiences, see Elizabeth Hillstrom, *Testing the Spirits* (Downers Grove, Ill.: InterVarsity Press, 1995), pp. 80-106.

Chapter 4: Reincarnation, Annihilation & Other Views
[1]John Snyder, *Reincarnation vs. Resurrection* (Chicago: Moody Press, 1984), p. 13.
[2]Tony Coffey, *Once a Catholic* (Eugene, Ore.: Harvest House, 1993), p. 140.

Chapter 5: Death by Choice
[1]Anne-Grace Scheinin, "The Burden of Suicide," *Newsweek*, February 7,

1983, p. 13.

[2]The story of Nazi "euthanasia" has been told powerfully by Michael Burleigh in *Death and Deliverance* (New York: Cambridge University Press, 1995).

Chapter 6: What Happens *After* I Die?

[1]James Watkins, *Death and Beyond* (Wheaton, Ill.: Tyndale House, 1993), pp. xiii, 207.

[2]I. Howard Marshall, *Commentary on Luke*, New International Greek Testament Commentary (Grand Rapids, Mich.: Eerdmans, 1978), p. 873.

Chapter 7: Hell

[1]From J. I. Packer's foreword to Ajith Fernando, *Crucial Questions About Hell* (Wheaton, Ill.: Crossway Books, 1991), p. x.

[2]Jesus used the word *Gehenna* eleven times in the Gospels: Matthew 5:22, 29, 30; 10:28; 18:9; 23:15, 33; Mark 9:43, 45, 47; and Luke 12:5. In each case he was referring to the final judgment of hell.

Chapter 9: Heaven

[1]This quotation and the narrative of Moody's death come from John Pollock, *Moody: The Biography* (Chicago: Moody Press, 1983), pp. 344-45.

[2]For an extensive study of what the Bible teaches about angels, see Douglas Connelly, *Angels Around Us* (Downers Grove, Ill.: InterVarsity Press, 1994).

Chapter 10: The Never-Ending Story

[1]Don Baker, *Heaven* (Portland, Ore.: Multnomah Press, 1983), n.p.

[2]I'm indebted to Don Baker for these categories (see ibid.).

Chapter 13: Comfort for Those Left Behind

[1]Joseph Bayly, *The Last Thing We Talk About* (Elgin, Ill.: David C. Cook, 1980), pp. 55-56.

Name & Subject Index

Scripture Index